AF430539

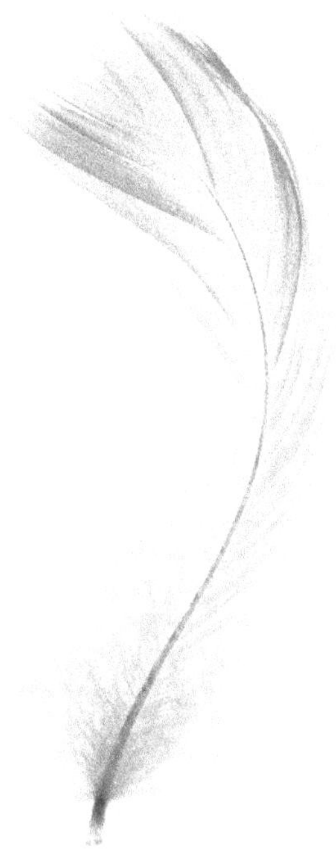

POETRY TAKES FLIGHT
Birds of California

James Roethe

Bird-in-Hand Publications

2023

Published by Bird-in-Hand Publications
Orinda, California

Softcover ISBN: 9798218102760
Hardcover ISBN: 9798218143213

Anna's Hummingbird sketch on the cover and title page by Nick Vaughn

Image credits on page vii

Book design and production by Lucky Valley Press
www.luckyvalleypress.com

Printed in the United States on acid-free paper

DEDICATION

To my Duende friends with whom I have spent many incredible hours hiking locally and through parts of Europe. As the only birder in our group, these friends have had to put up with my need to carry binoculars everywhere we have gone and to periodically interrupt discussions about the history of the areas where we hike with a question about a particular bird. They have also graciously endured my habit of circulating photos of all the birds I have seen during a trip, along with verbiage about where I saw each bird; my hope to instill in them a greater interest in birds and birding generally. While I may hope in vain, perhaps reading about some of our local birds in the form of poems, might further pique their interest in these wonders of nature.

CONTENTS

Acknowledgments vii

Epigraph viii

Preface ix

Acorn Woodpecker 3

American Crow 5

American Dipper 7

American Robin 9

Anna's Hummingbird 11

Bald Eagle 13

Belted Kingfisher 15

Bewick's Wren 17

Black Oystercatcher 19

Black Phoebe 21

Black-headed Grosbeak 23

Brant's Cormorant 25

Brewer's Blackbird 27

Brown Creeper 29

Brown-headed Cowbird 31

Bullock's Oriole 33

California Condor 35

California Quail 37

California Scrub Jay 39

California Thrasher 41

Cedar Waxwing 43

Chestnut-backed Chickadee 45

Cliff Swallow 47

Common Merganser 49

Common Poorwill 51

Common Raven 53

Dark-eyed Junco 55

Double Breasted Cormorant 57

European Starling 59

Golden Eagle 61

Great Horned Owl 63

The Gulls 65

Hermit Thrush 69

Killdeer 71

Lazuli Bunting 73

Lesser Goldfinch 75

Northern Shoveler 77

The Nuthatches.................................79

Nuttall's Woodpecker.........................83

Oak Titmouse 85

The Peeps....................................87

The Pelicans.................................89

Peregrine Falcon 93

The Phalaropes 95

Pileated Woodpecker.........................97

Pine Siskin 99

Red-breasted Sapsucker......................101

The Red Finches 103

Red-shouldered Hawk 107

Red-tailed Hawk.............................109

Red-winged Blackbird 111

The Ridgeway *(formerly "Clapper")* Rail......113

Ring-necked Duck............................115

Ring-necked Pheasant........................117

Ruby-crowned Kinglet........................119

Ruddy Duck 121

Sanderling 123

Snowy Plover................................125

Song Sparrow................................127

Stellar's Jay...............................129

Surf Scoter.................................131

The Teals 133

Turkey Vulture..............................135

Varied Thrush 137

Violet-green Swallow........................139

The Waders
  (Great Blue Heron and Great Egret) 141

Western Bluebird 143

Western Grebes 145

Western Meadowlark 149

Western Screech Owl.........................151

Western Tanager 153

White- and Gold-Crowned Sparrows 155

White-tailed Kites..........................159

White-throated Swift........................163

Wood Duck...................................165

Wood Warblers...............................167

Yellow-rumped Warbler 171

Afterword...................................172

About the Author 173

ACKNOWLEDGMENTS

I wish to thank Michael Bolte, Bob Lewis, Arthur Macmillan, Becky Matsubara, Doug Mosher, Ray Rozema and Peter Shen for graciously allowing me to use some of their amazing photographs of birds in this book, adding color and context to many of my poems. Each are local birders either in the East Bay or on the Monterey Peninsula as well as amateur photographers (all very good ones), who photograph birds locally and around the world. I confess to not being a good photographer and so I appreciate working with those who have honed their craft and produced the fine photos gracing *Poetry Takes Flight.* The book would not be the same without them and I am grateful for Michael, Bob, Mac, Becky, Doug, Ray and Peter for their assistance. (All photos for which the source is not identified were taken by the author or copied from open sources on the internet).

I would also like to thank my brother-in-law Nick Vaughn for the front cover sketch and the sketches gracing the interior and the back cover of the book. Nick is both a great artist and a birder who puts both of those talents together when sketching birds. Nick draws and birds in the vicinity around Albuquerque, New Mexico, where he lives.

Finally, I would like to thank Ginna and David Gordon of Lucky Valley Press for their invaluable assistance designing *Poetry Takes Flight* and helping me through the steps required to publish the book. I am indebted, indeed.

EPIGRAPH

"Everyone likes birds. What wild creature is more accessible to our eyes and ears, as close to us and everyone in the world, as universal as a bird?"

– Nature historian David Attenborough

"The very idea of a bird is a symbol and a suggestion to the poet. A bird seems to be at the top of the scale, so vehement and intense is his life, large-brained, large-lunged, hot, ecstatic, his frame charged with buoyancy and his heart with song."

– Naturalist John Burroughs

"Birds are an ecological litmus paper."

– Roger Tory Peterson

"The finch, the sparrow and the lark,
The plain-song cuckoo gray,
Whose note full many a man doth mark,
And dares not answer nay"

– William Shakespeare
A Midsummer Night's Dream, Act 3, scene 1

PREFACE

I am a bird watcher. Some would say I'm a birder or a twitcher, but let's go with bird watcher. I love to watch birds. I love birds. I took an interest in birds as a young boy but my primary interest at that time was butterflies and moths. There was a lady in the small town in Wisconsin where I grew up who collected butterflies and moths from all over the world. She also raised butterflies and moths at her home.

My fixation with butterflies and moths started when I found a large green moth on the windowsill of the home of a customer to whom I delivered newspapers. I gathered up the moth and took it home. A friend told me about the "Butterfly Lady" and suggested that I take the moth to her for identification. I did. I learned that it was Luna Moth and my exploration of butterflies, moths and nature began.

Years later, I took to walking my dog in the hills near home where I live with my wife in the East Bay region of San Francisco. I bought a book on butterflies and began to look for them during my walks. But there seemed to be so many different varieties, most of which looked nothing like those I chased during my youth. During these walks I began to notice the birds. They seemed more manageable and so I bought a bird book. The rest is history. I was hooked.

In my walks and travels I have identified over 750 species of birds—only a fraction of the 10,000 or so species that exist in the world. I have led bird walks, participated for many years in the annual Christmas bird count in my area and done some survey counts for the local Audubon Society. As I slipped into semi-retirement I also began to write— and have self-published several books about travel and my growing up experiences.

Recently, I thought it would be fun to combine my interest in writing and in birds. Hence, *Poetry Takes Flight.*

This is a book of short poems about birds. I had flirted with poetry in the past but thought now was the time to explore it more deeply with a subject I particularly enjoyed. I have selected as my subjects some of the more common birds seen where I walk several times each week in the hills near my home. Many of the poems are based on experiences I have had or seen with the bird at issue. For ease of reference, I have arranged the poems alphabetically by each of the bird's names rather than in taxonomic order – the order in which the birds would be featured in a typical field guide of today.

In Frank Delaney's book "Ireland," a "wise woman" tells a skeptic that writing and speaking poetry is simple. She is heard to say that a poet does not need stanzas or rhymes. Rather,

> "Every word that was ever spoken or sung has gone out into the air. They're all still up there. Oh, yes, they may be jumbled up but that's the beauty of the thing. Since words have their own lives, they can choose which other words they'll associate with. They're always looking for a good home, and a poem is about as good a home as a word can get.

> "By and large, words will arrange themselves. They may need a little help here and there to get settled into the right place in the right line and so on, but that's easily learned. What a poem needs by way of a good home is a heart of fire and a spirit of honor. Poems won't come to rest in a place of baseness. No self-respecting poem would think of entering a soul of perfidy."

She concludes by saying that the words of a poem "will come to you" "if you will only let them."

Perhaps that was true for the great Irish poets like Yeats, Heaney and Beckett. Perhaps to those poets the words simply "settled in the right place in the right line" with but a bit of molding by the poet to produce the poem. I, for one, found it a bit more difficult, taking a bit more time for the words to "settle in," and, even then, they've not always been quite the right words upon reflection. I don't profess to be a great poet. On the other hand, I hope that I have brought a bit of the "fire and spirit" to my poems so that a few of them, at least, merit a reread.

Despite the "wise woman's" admonition, some of my poems do have stanzas and are in various rhyming schemes. Others are in free verse. Free verse seems to be the fashion these days and so I have condescended in a few instances to write in free verse. However, I tend to be a bit of a traditionalist in the manner of Robert Frost (not a bad poet, most would say). Some of the poems are whimsical, some more serious. A few are written as Japanese Haiku (three lines of 5, 7 and 5, syllables, respectively, usually with a reference to nature or a season).

Blacking out the sun
Footprints left on sandy shore
Birder's enchantment

I hope, dear reader, that you will enjoy them.

  – Jim Roethe

POETRY TAKES FLIGHT

Acorn Woodpeckers are plentiful throughout most of California. They are large Woodpeckers with clown-like faces and they tend to be raucous— almost always heard before being seen. They get their name from their habit of storing acorns in holes they drill in dead or dying trees. Some of these trees are so riddled with holes there seems to be no place left for another, but the birds persist. These Woodpeckers created quite a commotion in one local community when they began to drill holes in the wooden eaves of some of the homes. Every year for the last several years, a family of Acorn Woodpeckers has been raised in the trees behind our house.

Acorn Woodpecker

Disliked by many–loud and noisy–rapping on their eaves
Reputation soiled for life to those you've failed to please
But I see it quite differently, though raucous you might be
You are pleasing to the eye and bring ample joy to me

White patches on your wings and tail show clearly as you fly
Red crown and clownish face are sure to catch the eye
of those who hold you dear, no pest or nuisance you
But rather something special, your cloak a lovely hue

Wherever I am apt to go, to park or nearby woods
Or even trees so bountiful, in my own neighborhood
I hear then see you go about the daily chores you do
Preparing for the winter's clime when food supplies are few

On walks through lush Briones' hills, I never fail to pass
The snag of ancient ash or oak, upon which you've amassed
The largest horde of winter food–abundant acorns cached
More than you can ever need, a tribute to your craft

Come spring, it's a delight to see that idle you've been not
For there upon my Alder tree, three fledglings stately sit
Somewhere nearby a family raised, it's happened every year
No mind their loud cacophony, a sound I love to hear

American Crows have the reputation of being noisy, always in medium to large flocks, and smart. All are true. I have seen 85 or more crows cavorting on my local golf course during annual Christmas bird counts. And beware the bag of chips you picked up at the tenth hole snack shack as you navigate to the next hole. It is also the rare occurrence where I see a "murder" of crows before I hear them. As a member of the Corvid family, they are known to be among the smartest of birds. A family of 10 or 12 Crows reside near my home in Orinda, California. On Sundays, I replenish my feeders and leave a bit of corn on the ground for the Crows and Jays. The Crows are invariably waiting.

Photo by Becky Matsubara

American Crow

Dark wings aflutter
Wind blowing through drying stalks
Crows well fed tonight

Black shadows in trees
Time for feeding feathered friends
Patience rewarded

Birds hover on high
New mown grass and well-shaped greens
Seeds and insects thrive

Snack at turn on ten
Oak trees in full foliage
Theft is short and swift

Photo by Peter Shen

American Dippers are small gray birds that post themselves in running streams to catch tiny insects and arachnids floating past them in the water. They have strong legs, wings and toes that let them "walk" underwater to catch their prey. They prefer clear, fast flowing mountain streams, but on one occasion, I observed a dipper in a city park foraging on the smallest rill of a stream. Very unusual.

American Dipper

A stroll through Laguna Grande Park on a sunny day
Checking out the birds near the pond along my way
As I strode along the path, past verboten woods
Hoping that a kinglet or a Townsend's warbler would
Condescend to show itself close by to where I stood

My attention being redirected by a gurgling sound
I noticed that a little rill of water slowly wound
Aside the path on which I sauntered as I searched for birds
No wider than a yardstick, for depth its width one third
But as I gazed along its course, I soon was lost for words

For there atop a meager rock, its tail a bobbing shaft
A Dipper doing its utmost to set about its craft
Lunging for a spider that afloat did pass him by
Then diving under water in pursuance of a fly
This small gray bird oblivious to every passerby

But why, I asked, was Dipper deign to forage in this place
No rushing mountain stream one deems a normal Dipper base
But just a tiny rill no more than thirty meters long
Not a place that birders would say this bird belongs
Yet deep inside I hope and pray its stay it will prolong

Photo by Becky Matsubara

The American Robin is a familiar bird across the United States. This poem is based on my childhood memories in Wisconsin where the Robin is the state bird and where the first Robin of the new year was always a sign that spring had officially arrived.

American Robin

Most common bird of summer clime,
I deign to see you in your prime
Scratching under forest's crown
For insects neath the leafy ground

Come fall as leaves turn orange and red
You blend into the forest, spread
before you with its outstretched arms
Your haven from approaching storms

As snow portends winter's approach
You fatten up so as to cope
With that long journey you'll soon take
To warmer lands, the cold to shake

But now a stirring deep inside
Compels return to seek your bride
For me, return means but one thing
I see you, harbinger of spring

Numerous Anna's Hummingbirds live year-round in the garden behind my home. They are the most common hummingbird in these parts. This poem describes some of their antics ranging from their competition at the feeder to their courtship flight whereby they soar into the air and then hurtle downward forming a curve like the letter "J" on their descent. My Anna's love my feeders but also feast on the many Salvias planted behind our house and drink from my fountain, sometimes hovering over the bubbling water while doing so.

Photo by Becky Matsubara

Anna's Hummingbird

What is that whirring noise I hear
The faintest "tic" upon my ear
A flash of green and white and red
Toward the blaze of flowers ahead
As if suspended o'er the brink
It hovers by and by to drink
The sweetest nectar God has made
To fuel its frantic escapades

Then suddenly with warning none
A beeline up toward clouds and sun
Then back to earth with wings afire
In hopes of kindling love's desire
But should a brother come its way
In fierce pursuit he's chased away
No matter whether big or small
To Anna's, matters not at all

I marvel at the sight I see
When Anna deigns to honor me
With flights of fancy in my sight
This tiniest of God's delights
Darting off twixt flower and flower
Floating, yet with awesome power
Beauty, strength, fragile but bold
There to marvel, love, behold

Photo by Becky Matsubara

The Bald Eagle is our national bird. It is not common in Northern California but seen from time to time. They feed primarily on fish they catch in their strong talons or steal from another bird. On one occasion during a Christmas bird count, while having our lunch on the deck of our leader's home, we looked up and saw three Bald Eagles cavorting high above us—two adults and a juvenile. It was glorious to see.

Bald Eagle

Photo by Becky Matsubara

Our national bird
Waves of ripening grain
Born we to be free

Soaring high above
Ice beginning to melt
No hunger tonight

Black and white symbol
Sun shining through silky clouds
A country at peace

Sharp talons, strong beak
River approaching the sea
The Salmon suffers

Virtually every lake, small pond or year-round stream in Northern California has hosted one or two Belted Kingfishers over the last several years. I have counted as many as three during my annual Christmas counts in the North Oakland area. Wherever there is abundant fresh water and fish, there will be Kingfishers. They perch in trees along the bank and, when a fish is sited, dive headlong into the water. Their harsh rattle of a song can be heard year-round throughout the U.S. with the exception of our extreme southwest deserts. Unlike most bird species, the female is more colorful than the male—sporting a rusty breast band below her steel gray collar.

Kingfisher – Male   Photo by Bob Lewis

Belted Kingfisher

Most unusual bird of our near lakes and ponds
Female more attractive, she no demimonde
Hers the addition of a rusty breast band
His a dull breast of pure white, rather bland

Master of fishing you were bred to be
Watching aloft from atop a near tree
Only rarely you miss when the water is clear
Eye of an Eagle 'til prey dost appear

Then like a bullet that's fired from a gun
Intent on your purpose, your target to stun
You shoot into action, take aim at your foe
Headlong you hurtle t'ward target below

Piercing the water you alight with a splash
Wings folded inward, your long bill does grasp
The fish you intended, wriggling to be free
But your grasp is secure and it is not to be

I watch you in wonder as you survey the lake
Searching for perches, and make no mistake
Find the best ones you will; for this task you've a flair
You're a fisher par excellence – pecheur extraordinaire

Kingfisher – Female
Photo by Becky Matsubara

Photo by Becky Matsubara

*My wife describes many of the birds I point out to her as being simply "little brown birds."
I tell her there is much more to see of these "little brown birds" if she would just take
a look through my binoculars. So, I simply had to write one poem about "little brown
birds" and the wren seemed the perfect candidate.*

Bewick's Wren

Little Brown Bird
I see you from afar
You forage in my garden
But what are you really?
I see only
a little brown bird

Come closer
Better for me to see
Will you fly if I approach?
A friend says: wait! Try these
I raise them to my eyes
My world is changed

You are brown – that is true
But your breast is lighter
I see a bright flash of white
above each eye
And when your tail is raised
As it often is
The pattern of black stripes is clear
running its entire course

Yes, you are a Little Brown Bird
But you are much more than that
You are a Wren, and proud to be

As you might imagine, Black Oystercatchers love oysters. In fact, any mollusk will do. They hunt on the rocky shores of California, the Northwest and Alaska for mussels and other mollusks exposed when the tide goes out. I often see these Oystercatchers when walking along coastal trails in the Monterey Peninsula Area. All black, except for their bright red-orange bill and red eyes, they look surreal yet are easy to spot, most often in groups of two or three. When flushed they give out a harsh "yuk, yuk, yuk," that can be heard for long distances. Their American Oystercatcher sister inhabits the east and gulf coasts.

Photo by Becky Matsubara

Black Oystercatcher

Most peculiar of birds
Clings to coastal rocks
Black as the blackest night
A phantom, a paradox

With your long, sharp bill
Like the reddest sunset sky
Cold eyes of same said hue
An apparition in disguise

As fate would have it so
There thrives on coastal shore
What Nature has bestowed
And phantom bird adores

From predators it's safe
Its shell as armor strong
The lowly mussel clings
In clusters, mighty throngs

Secure in their belief
That armor keeps them safe
Open as tides engulf
Clamped tight as tides abate

But Oystercatcher's bill
Efficient to the max
With little effort lost
Does mussel soon dispatch
Yes, that curious reddish bill
Fully adapted to the task

Photo by Becky Matsubara

Black Phoebes, small members of the flycatcher family, are all black except for their belly and under tail coverts which are snow white. Black Phoebes are common year-round and all through the Bay Area—both near the coast and inland—where they perch on branches, fence posts or weed stalks and then dart out to catch insects in the air, usually returning to their same perch. They are efficient at their task.

Black Phoebe

How delicate and fragile you do seem
Balanced on that slimmest stalk or reed
Little it does bend as you await
Your prey to pass nearby to meet its fate

No Titan you, daughter of earth and sky
Battling with Olympian gods on high
But rather simple creature born below
Survive each day your only battle known

In Greece you are the "radiant, shining one"
Of Brightness you, of luster like the sun
An apt description of your image fair
Beauty of ivory and ebony laid bare

When e'er I see you I am duly struck
Your diligence, your patience and your pluck
Ever to the task, your burden clear
Though delicate you are, you never veer
So admire you I must, I you endear

To my mind, the song of the male Black-headed Grosbeak is as good as bird songs come. A bit similar to the warbling of the American Robin, the Grosbeak adds an extra flare—a sweeter and lovelier sound that reverberates through the woods where these birds sing from the high canopies of the trees. During my many walks, I often hear Robins singing at all times of the year. Come early spring, I keep a sharp listen in the hopes of distinguishing the call of the early arrival Grosbeaks. Then I know that spring has finally arrived.

Photo by Becky Matsubara

Black-headed Grosbeak

I eagerly await your return each year
You'll be here come early spring
I'm looking forward to your return
Your glorious voice – Sing to me

Briones' trails a half-hour hence
I search the heights of trees I pass
Keep a keen ear, lest you call
Your glorious voice – Sing to me

When traipsing Tilden's vast expanse
Along the trail by Wildcat Stream
I strain to hear your warbling whistle
Your glorious voice – Sing to me

More pure than Robin's likened song
Your slow and steady pace
Makes heart strings jump a bit when heard
Your glorious voice – Sing to me

As lovely as you are to me
Orange breast, black head and back
In mind they pale when once I hear
Your glorious voice – Sing to me

The Brant's Cormorant is the largest of the cormorants that live off the Northern California coast. They are strictly salt-water birds although they rarely venture far from the shore. Huge numbers of these cormorants live in colonies on rocky islands near the coast. Bird Rock at Point Lobos State Natural Reserve, south of Carmel, California, contains one of those colonies. It is there that they breed, free of land predators. The idea for this poem is based on a recent feeding frenzy seen near Monterey, where a shoal of anchovies congregated near the surface of the water, attracting a large variety of birds and sea mammals.

Brant's Cormorant

Water roiling, birds aflutter, "seals and otters too," I mutter
All attempt to get their share of what I'm seeing just off shore
From above some birds are diving, from below the seals are striving
They to gather fish are thriving, feed themselves and those ashore
Chicks resignedly awaiting
For a meal and nothing more

Chief among this mass commotion, habitants of coastal ocean
Cormorants, of species Brant's, do hunt for those they do adore
Chicks on yonder rocks assemble, snow white fluffs of fur resemble
Waiting patiently they tremble, Mom come knocking at the door
With the gifts they've been awaiting
Yes, a meal and nothing more

Feeding frenzy finally ended, birds return as they intended
Chicks with open mouths awaiting, parents back as they'd foresworn
Colony of hundreds strong, fill the rocks in copious throng
Where they've bred for eons long, just as myriad times before
Wheel of life is yet enduring
Stills the waters evermore

Brewer's Blackbirds are common and widespread throughout California and the Northwest both in rural areas and in our cities and towns. Males are a glossy black but for an almost iridescent yellow eye. Females are a dull gray-brown. Like other Blackbirds, they congregate in flocks and are common residents of open country. As they feed principally on insects, they tend to be plentiful near farms and feedlots where the cattle's feet are continuously churning up the soil and the manure produced by the cattle attracts a wide variety of insects. But truth be told, these birds will eat anything. The next time you dine at your favorite outdoor restaurant, look around to see if one of those birds picking up scraps dropped from the table might be a Brewer's Blackbird. It could very well be

Brewer's Blackbird

Bird of fields, farms and parking lots
It's a fact; not finicky you
Equally comfy in each such spot
Almost any such place will do

At home in the dairy farm's placid field
Or aside a pile of manure
Or in the town by a restaurant
Both have an equal allure

As long as there is a morsel to eat
Contented you will be
Insects or seeds, bread crumbs or meat
All do appeal to thee

Where ever you are, you strut around
Always in search of food
Picking and pecking at all morsels found
Downward your eyes are glued

And speaking of eyes, yours yellow glow
A contrast to body black
Eyes so lustrous that all will know
It's a Brewer's going after that snack
For food scraps, you have quite a knack

Now please do not think lesser of me
'cause food seems all that I crave
It's just that o'er time I have come to be
So skilled at the talents God gave

Brown Creepers are that little mottled brown bird seen in any of our local woods climbing up the trunk of trees looking for insects and spiders. They climb up the trunk using their tail as an anchor, usually encircling the trunk as they go, and when they reach the top, fly to the bottom of an adjacent tree and repeat the process. They have a thin decurved bill useful for prying insects from under the bark.

Brown Creeper

That piece of bark that's come to life
Unseen until with movement quick
A frantic need to upward climb
While from the bark it probes and pricks

Focused on the task at hand
This tiny ball of feathers fair
Dissuaded not from what he's planned
Completes his task with utmost care

Then down he flies from lofty perch
To forest floor where there awaits
Another oak whose scaly bark
Invites another upward race

No creature could more busy be
Than lowly Creeper hard at work
Provides for self and family
A job, a calling, not a quirk
A calling Creeper dare not shirk

Cowbirds are often looked down on by the birding community because they are "brood parasites." This means they lay their eggs in the nests of other birds who go on to raise the chicks as their own. The Cowbird chick often pushes the foster parents' chicks out of the nest, where they become prey to predators. Still the foster parents continue to raise and fledge their intruder. Cowbirds are birds of open country, so named because they forage in fields where cattle graze. They reside in the non-mountainous regions of California year-round. In the winter, they often flock with other blackbird species, sometimes in quite large flocks. And guess what? The males have a brown head.

Photo by Arthur Macmillan

Brown-headed Cowbird

Lover of open country
An enigma you
Forest gave way to field
Your numbers grew and grew

Eye-catching brown
atop glossy black
Sets you apart
From the Blackbird pack

But as each rose has thorns
Your misdemeanor clear
You lay your precious eggs
In other's nests each year
Your chicks for them to rear

Good parents you are not
Let meadowlark or wren
Fulfill parental chores
For you, time and again

No wonder you are not
A favorite of those
Who love and cherish birds
The thorn on this fair rose

The Bullock's Oriole is a summer resident of Northern California but it makes me think of fall. This, because of its color—orange and black—the colors of Halloween. It is a beautiful bird, but with a harsh song. It is found a bit inland from the coast, inhabiting large Oak and Sycamore trees where the climate is a bit warmer and dryer. Its nest, like that of other Orioles, consists of woven plant material that hangs from a tree branch. It favors fruit and insects but will also forage at flowers and hummingbird feeders for nectar.

Bullock's Oriole

Nest soft as velvet
Perfectly crafted
by an expert weaver
Hangs delicately from the tree
Sways softly in the breeze

Home to beautiful birds
The colors of autumn
Yet with us through the spring
And summer only
Few more beautiful than you

Why then your harsh call
An insult to your beauty
Still, your partner answers
To her, a siren's call
Consumed by love
She nears

Chirping from the nest
Cries of the hungry
For them you bring insects
The protein they need to grow
For you the nectar of the poppies
and wild daisies will suffice

Gone too soon
Our southern neighbors to enjoy
Your beauty, whilst I wait
For spring and your return
Your colors once again
To remind me of fall

Drawing by Nick Vaughn

Photo by Doug Mosher

The California Condor is North America's largest bird with a wing-span approaching 10 feet. It is also one of the rarest, listed as "critically endangered" under federal law. In 1985, there were believed to be only five adult birds left in the wild thanks to deaths caused primarily by environmental pollution, poison bait and lead fragments in carcasses the birds ate. Successful captive breeding programs at the San Diego Wild Animal Park and the Los Angeles Zoo brought these numbers up and, in 1991, the first captive bred Condor was reintroduced into the wild. As of 2020, there were 504 California Condors in the wild, having been reintroduced in Arizona, Utah and California in the United States and in Mexico's Baja Peninsula. Four juvenile California Condors will soon be released into the wild in Northern California. It is hoped that their range will eventually expand into the Northwest states of Oregon, Washington and Idaho.

California Condor

Largest of our native birds
Symbol of the wild
Deified by cave art's words
Mankind to beguile

Nature's cleaning crew they say
Shouldn't cause them harm
Yet, man has seemed to find a way
The cause of great alarm

Nearly have become extinct
Through the fault of man
Soon at home throughout the West
From Baja to Spokane

Spirit of our native peoples
Miwok, Mono, Khiz
Thought of you as God or Devil
Ganesha or Eris

Largest of our native birds
Flying ever free
Soaring o'er us fearlessly
Evermore to see

Ganesha – Hindu God of Benevolence.
Eris – Greek Goddess of Discord.

The California Quail is California's state bird. It is found in most temperate regions of the state, unlike its cousins the Gambel's Quail (a desert bird) and the Mountain Quail (found only at higher elevations). Unlike most birds, baby Quail leave their nest shortly after hatching and can be seen in brushy woods and chaparral areas following closely behind their parents. They are cute, to say the least. Most Quail have a "topknot" extending from the top of their head. In the case of the California Quail, it is curved. The male's call is nasal and loud, echoing over the terrain in the hopes of attracting a mate. For some time, we had a covey of California Quail in our back yard, sometimes perching on our deck.

Photo by Peter Shen

California Quail

California's bird
Golden summer hills glowing
Sun and sea abound

Patter of small feet
Dawn breaks over Chaparral
Family happiness

Call resounds off hills
New spring flowers bursting forth
Love is in the air

Quail on fence post sits
Stream coursing through brushy tract
There's no place like home

A few years ago, the Western Scrub Jay populations were split into two separate species based on differences that emerged over time. Thus, the California Scrub Jay. These Jays are loud and scrappy and smart. They get their way at my feeders. When hungry they will soar in, frighten all the other birds away and have their fill.

California Scrub Jay

"Shek, Shek, Shek, Shek, Shek, I hear your soulful cry
Always let me know you're near, as I am passing by
Among the smartest birds on earth, the humble Jay, it's said
Ever seeks advantage, so as to get ahead

I watch you from my window, feeding on the corn
I've place there for the squirrels, so as to keep them from
What's meant for smaller song birds who'll brighten up my day
But soon the corn is gone, so squirrels have their way
You Jays have spoiled my plan, to keep meddlers at bay

But that is just your nature, grabbing what you see
Always on alert to find a source of energy
Be it corn or other seeds, organic matter, too
As long as it is edible, gladly you make it do

You also seem a bully, when feeders catch your eye
You rush to get your share, causing other birds to fly
Care not that you have frightened your brethren big and small
You calmly go about your task, bothered not at all

Despite your reputation, a bully though you be
The benefit of doubt, I'll always give to thee
You are one of God's creatures, put on this earth with us
Assume must I, a plan God had, so who am I to fuss

The California Thrasher is a year-round resident of California west of the Sierra Nevada, excluding the hot Central Valley. It gets its name from its long, decurved bill it uses to "thrash" the ground in search of insects and other goodies. It is not often seen but one knows when it is near from its cacophony of short scratchy notes, often repeated two or three times before squeaking out another different guttural note which also is repeated. It belongs to the Mimidae Family known for their diverse songs which often mimic the notes of other species.

Photo by Becky Matsubara

California Thrasher

What is that strident sound I hear
Its most offensive to my ear
Brassy and shrill, repetitive too
Enough to drive a man cuckoo

On second thought I ponder the source
Nothing mechanical or coarse
No squeaky wheel the author be
Rather, a bird both wild and free

I gaze upon this creature wild
Long decurved bill as if defiled
But for this bird a useful tool
To scratch the ground, for Thrasher's fuel

Now that I know from whence sounds came
I do not hear those sounds the same
their harshness softened to my ear
Sweeter the squeals and squeaks appear

The moral of this clever tale
Take time before you do bewail
What seems at first adverse to be
Looks different, when "the whole" you see

Photo by Bob Lewis

Cedar Waxwing are winter visitors to the Bay Area, always in large flocks. Now they're here, now they're gone. Only during the short summer months, while in Northern Canada, do they pair up for breeding. Find a tree or bush loaded with berries and sooner or later, you will see these birds, lovers of berries. Named after a waxy red blotch on the end of certain of their wings, these grayish birds also sport a short crest, a black face mask, and the smallest splotch of yellow on the end of their tail feathers.

Cedar Waxwing

It's late fall and the berries are thick
on the Pyracantha off my back deck
The Robins and Thrush are getting their fill
Seems not to matter, most berries do still
Cling to that bush on the side of my hill

The Thrush is a loner, the Robins a pair
Not much they can do to denude that bush fair
'Twould take a battalion of birds to do that
Large cadre of soldiers ready for combat
To strip all those berries, no army ersatz

But what is that rustling out by the trees
A full corps of soldiers aloft on the breeze
Making a beeline where berries are found
Attacking those berries – 'tis something profound
And doing it silently, nary a sound

Now finally sated, they roost in the trees
I see their short crests, their black masks, with
   ease
Yellow on tail and red blotch on the wing
As if dipped by an artist (the strangest of things)
In her palette of colors, of wonders wellspring

This legion of birds, it soon will depart
Perhaps they'll return next year at the start
Of that season when berries again become ripe
To again attack bushes, their intent to swipe
Then vanish again, away into the night

Photo by Becky Matsubara

The Chestnut-backed Chickadee is one of the most common birds where I live. I recall a visit by a relative from Albuquerque who went birding with me at one of my local patches. I spotted a Chickadee and directed his attention to it. "Oh, a common Black-capped Chickadee" he exclaimed. When I pointed out that it was in fact a Chestnut-backed Chickadee, a bird he had never seen, he was ecstatic, exclaiming that it was a "lifer" for him. He also observed that whenever we saw a Chickadee, it seemed that other birds were nearby. Thus, this poem.

Photo by Becky Matsubara

Chestnut-backed Chickadee

Most common bird seen every time
I venture thru this patch of mine
Your chatter lets me know you're near
A song I always love to hear
A song that brings me joy and cheer

Your chestnut back sets you apart
From cousins that are strewn throughout
The northern woods and eastern plain
The southern deserts, mountain chain
It's California where you reign

When you are near there seem to be
Abundant others foraging
In flocks of different species who
are seeming to be following you
and emulating what you do

But hear you first, your "tsidi-cheer-cheer"
Brings to attention those who near
the spot where you hold forth for all
to marvel at you as you call
notes echoing through forest tall

My outings walking yonder hills
Seem never to be quite fulfilled
If your sweet song I somehow miss
Your gift to me like nature's kiss
That puts me in a state of bliss

A number of years ago, the club to which I belong built a new tennis building overlooking Lake Cascade, the lake created by the damming of Lauterwasser Creek to provide water for the club's golf course. A year after the facilities were built, a "Gulp" of Cliff Swallows decided that the eave of the new tennis facility was the perfect place to build their nests that year. Not only was it near the lake with its abundance of insects, but also the golf course where these Swallows could be seen cruising over the fairways grabbing any bug, spider or fly within reach.

Photo by Becky Matsubara

Photo by Bob Lewis

Cliff Swallows live in colonies and build nests of mud not only on cliffs, but also under the eaves of buildings, under bridges and anywhere else where a protected cleft on rock or in or on a building can be found. They tend to return to the same nesting site year after year. While lovely birds, the initial outcry from club members was loud and swift as the birds did what all birds do on the decking around the tennis building. As the club's "birdman," I was tasked with finding a solution. This poem is based on that experience.

Cliff Swallow

Look at the mess they are making
  A member said to me
Droppings all over the windows
  Through which I can hardly see

When I come for a game of tennis
  And to gaze out at yon Lake Cascade
I expect cleanliness at our premises
  To walk 'round the decks unafraid

"Let's get rid of those pesky swallows"
  The only solution, he said
Knock the nests down in the eaves
  To assure that the birds will have fled

No, no, I protested aloud
  Those birds have the right to live
A better solution I've found
  A compromise I'll surely give

To achieve this, you must have patience
  These things can't be done overnight
"They're breeding." It calls for complacence
  A year, then they'll be out of sight

The fledges all flown from the coop
  Parents winging their way to the south
Time to put plan in action, to dupe
  those Swallows when next they turn north

Nests taken down from the eaves
  Netting to prevent them anew
When encountered they'll know they're deceived
  But what will the poor Swallows do

It is April and birds are returning
  To the same place they nested last year
Their scouts have arrived and are yearning
  For their home, so the Lake they'll be near

For abundance of insects that hover
  Over water where many were bred
A perfect home base they've discovered
  So their chicks will be adequately fed

By golly, they've found a solution
  Under building they'll build their new nests
All happy for their ablution
  For both man and bird worked out best

The Swallows live still by the Lake
  Where abundance of food can be found
And the Members, their ground strokes they make
  Without worry – It's best all around

Now members and Swallows as neighbors
  Reside happily side by side
Every year birds return to their capers
  Members marvel at Swallows with pride

Photo by Peter Shen

Common Mergansers are just that—"common" wherever there is fresh water. They are diving ducks with serrated edges on their bills that help them grab and hold onto prey when they dive for a meal, sometime referred to as "Sawbills." In the winter, when they are most present where I live, they tend to form large flocks, as many as 30 or 40 strong, which together look like an armada as they patrol the lake, pond or reservoir where they can be seen.

Common Merganser

Denizen of local ponds, a diving duck you be
Also seen along the coast where river meets the sea
Or resting on a glassy lake, far inland suits you fine
And even rushing rivers offer favorable clime

And so I think it fair to say, particular you're not
As long as there is water near, a person's likely aught
To see you resting many strong, flotilla so they say
Or battling the waters rush as you fight the angry spray

I see you when at Tahoe, in kayak near the shore
When casting flies on Yellowstone, amidst the river's roar
Or hiking by the reservoir, along San Pablo Trail
Or during annual Christmas counts at nearby Lake Cascade
It seems no matter what the source, fresh water you will brave

Distinct green head of male contrasts with snowy sides and breast
His lady friend a drabber gray nevertheless is blessed
With rusty head and nape and neck, her head always held high
She ever strikes a handsome pose as flock goes floating by

A winter bird you are to those throughout my neighborhood
The time of year you congregate, "like soldiers," if you would
Ofttimes as much as forty strong, an armada so they say
Sailing o'er the water clear on lake or pond or bay
I marvel as you pass me by, another wondrous day

Common Poorwill belong to that group of nocturnal insect eaters (Nighthawks, Nightjars, Poorwill and Whip-poor-will) collectively referred to as "goatsuckers;" this from the early (and false) belief that these birds would fly into barns at night and suckle on goats. They are small, with mottled black and white backs that blend in with the branches and ground on which they perch. While appearing to have a small bill, their open mouth is quite large and filled with stiff bristles that help them catch and hold on to the insects they catch in flight.

Common Poorwill

You're on that branch just a few feet away
I see you not
God given camo' keeps predators at bay
Unhappy lot

A hunter by night, you excel at your task
A stalker you
Perched on the ground, 'til an insect does pass
You await your due

Spring upward you, toward prey you might catch
Assailant fair
Your victim high above you soon dispatch
Out of midair

That silly rumor folks ascribe to you
Of goats and such
While fun to tell it simply is not true
Of truth not much

You feed only on insects in the air
The night patrolled
To suggest otherwise would not be fair
Truth must be told

Photo by Peter Shen

This poem is in remembrance of a summer at my home during which a pair of Ravens nested in a Pine Tree behind our home and fledged four chicks. Naturally, the meter is to Poe's "The Raven."

Common Raven

Lustrous black of night reminding, as I watch my wits unwinding
Mouth agape as it goes flying flashing past my kitchen door
Then alights near yonder willow, looks aloft t'ward clouds that billow
High above adjacent hill where pines adorn the hillock floor
Must be something there I mutter
Just the trees and nothing more

Then burst of speed with wings aflutter, soaring skyward as I utter
Must be something else up yonder, something precious, something more
Makes this bird sail high aloft, to a place secure and soft
Is there something there which oft, welcomes home through nature's door
What can it be, "a nest" I wonder
Waiting there, his paramour

O'er next few weeks no time to waste, back and forth with anxious haste
Black bird and mate seem in a chase, to shore up what they're aiming for
Who are this couple in their fury, always seeming in a hurry
Back and forth to nest they scurry, what is it they have in store
Must be of the most importance
Drudges they to very core

Soon loud croaking sounds asunder, filling air with sounds of wonder
Fledges soaring while I ponder, whether numbering three or four
Soon they're gone young Raven fledglings, off to seek out different dwellings
Nest abandoned parents calling, no response does echo forth
Hope to see more come next summer
Phantom birds loved evermore

Drawing by Nick Vaughn

The Dark-eyed Junco is the first bird that piqued my interest in birding as an adult. During many walks near my home, I kept seeing this brown bird with a bit of white in its outer tail feathers. Curiosity caused me to buy my first Field Guide for Western Birds. Ironically, the guide was written by David Allen Sibley, the namesake of the regional park where I first noticed this bird.

Dark-eyed Junco Feeding Fledges

Dark-eyed Junco

Despite its name, a sparrow he,
Ubiquitous from sea to sea
The bird that caught my interest
When first seen I'd ne'er have guessed
A life-long passion, daily pressed

A walk through Sibley's wilderness
A bit of exercise my quest
Across my trail small birds careen,
White flash in tail feathers seen
"What are those birds- so swift and lean"

Piqued curiosity became
"I'll need a guide to learn bird's name"
So off to nature store I dashed,
A field guide so at long last
This bird's "handle" I'd know if asked

A Junco from the book I learned
Quite common here said book confirmed
Black hood and brownish back and sides
White in tail the Junco hides
Until in flight white hits one's eyes

Now that I have this book in hand
The joy of birding does command
That I go out and search the hills
For other birds whose sighting will
Instill in me God-given thrills

The moral of this quirky tale
The lowly Junco has prevailed
In bringing birding's gift to me
A gift that will forever be
A source of joy that sets me free

Photo by Becky Matsubara

Double-crested Cormorants are the only Cormorants that frequent inland waters and can be found throughout the United States. They also nest in large rookeries with Great Blue Herons and Great Egrets high in trees near water. I see them often near where I live and in areas near the Monterey Peninsula where I have a second home. The rookery at Elkhorn Slough can be raucous during the breeding season.

Double Breasted Cormorant

Bird of coastal waters, inland ponds and lakes
Arrayed like soldiers by the rocky shore
Standing sentinel 'til water's surface shakes
Roiling, shimmering, anchovies galore

Then fly you in formation, water low
Barely o'er the glimmering water breached
One before the other, in a row
Until the angry fishing grounds are reached.

At rest in all the trees 'round Lake Cascade
Wings outstretched to dry out in the sun
Then to the water, fishing flair displayed
Fulfill your needs and then when fishing's done
It's back to roost with wings again outflung

As spring approaches, time to gather all
At roosts with nearby waters left behind
In Eucalyptus trees amidst the thrall
Of Herons, Egrets, others of your kind

Soon scores of nests in that small stand of trees
Burst forth with life and squawking soon begins
The noise though sharp and harsh does set you free
Signals new life, one more of Nature's wins

In every nook and cranny o'er this land
You make your being known by presence fair
So all who see you fast will understand
Appreciate your genius, your flair

European Starlings were introduced in America in or around 1860 when 100 or so of the birds were released in New York's Central Park. They are now ubiquitous across the nation, estimated to be 200 million strong. A member of the Blackbird family, they are considered a pest in some places when hundreds roost in town or village trees making both a racket and a mess for the town folks. They are known to congregate in large flocks, sometimes thousands strong. When they take to the air in what is called a murmuration, they are known to create fantastic images across the early evening sky.

Photo by Becky Matsubara

European Starling

Dark cloud aswirl o'er the sky
First a huge balloon
Now a whale afloat on azure sea
Changing, ever changing
Moving together
Like fish swarming o'er a reef
Ebbing and flowing,
First up, then down, then forward
As if one

Like the Passenger Pigeon of yore
But not so abundant
The sky is not blackened
Rather, you paint an inky wave
Across the horizon
Beautiful to see,
Hard to forget

Yet come nightfall
Time to roost and rest
Still hundreds strong
Protection in numbers
Your beauty wanes
For those who pass below
Until the 'morrow
When you will rise in flight again
Beautiful once more

The majestic Golden Eagle is an uncommon, but year-round, resident of the U.S. west of the Rocky Mountains. Of interest, it also inhabits parts of Europe and Asia. It is truly an international bird. It is a bird of the open country where it hunts prey as large as jackrabbits. It will also take snakes, birds and carrion. In the adult, it's "golden head" is often hard to see against its dark brown back and breast.

Juvenile Golden Eagle   Photo by Arthur Macmillan

Golden Eagle

Wings uplifted, well you soar
High above the valley floor
O'er the hills and mountains high
Mighty monarch of the sky

Robust hunter that you are
Apex predator savoir
On alpine thermal winds you waft
'til prey you see from high aloft

With folded wings you hurtle down
Torpedo like with ne'er a sound
Toward unsuspecting mouse or vole
Raptorial bird on patrol

On aerie cliffs you make your home
With ample space for you to roam
O'er nearby hills and valleys low
O'er mountaintops and high plateaus
Fulfill your needs your life's seeds sown

I glory at your majesty
Your golden crown worn gallantly
Dominant o'er all you see
Commander of your destiny

The Great-horned Owl is the largest of the owls in our area. During the late winter and early spring, I hear them calling in the Pines behind our house and beyond. They hunt at night. Their wings are arrayed in such a way that they cannot be heard in flight. Sometimes during a walk in the surrounding hills, I will accidentally flush a Great-horned Owl. It is something to behold.

Photo by Becky Matsubara

Great Horned Owl

Silent hunter of the night
I hear you from the stand of pine two doors down
But never see you

You are a ghost in the night.
Hunting quietly o'er the meadow behind the house
And in the Oak dotted hills that lay beyond

Wings spread wide, wider than I am tall
Feathers perfectly arrayed so prey know not what hit them
Until it is too late

A big bird; who would think could hunt so silently
Surely not the squirrel behind our house
or the unsuspecting vole in the field beyond

Yet in early morn, when the hunt is over and you securely on your roost
I hear the faint, but clear "hoo, hoo, hoooo that tells me you are near
Again I search in vain to see you

Silent hunter of the night,
I am comforted when I know you're near
You are surely a ghost, but you are my ghost

Western Gull

We often see Gulls along beaches, lakes, rivers and even gathered in fields where they forage for insects. Most people just say, "Oh look! Seagulls." Be that as it may, there is no bird whose common name is "Seagull." Rather, there are a wide variety of "gulls" that inhabit our shores, lakes and fields. Each a bit different. Some bigger than others. Some with dark black backs, some light gray and some grayer still. Some with yellow bills and some with dark bills. The yellow-billed kind may show either a black or red spot at the tip of its bill, or both. All of this fails to account for the fact that juvenile gulls look entirely different and can take two or three years to morph into adult plumage. Never let it be said that identifying gulls is easy.

The Gulls

Look there, it's a Seagull she proudly proclaimed
As she ran o'er the beach, then heard me exclaim
No bird by that name has ever been found
A "gull" surely yes, but "Seagulls" don't abound

There's Bonaparte's, Western, Laughing and Mew
Ring-billed, Franklin's and Little Gulls, too
California, Herring and Ross also here
But nary a "Seagull," do I make myself clear

Black-headed, Glaucous-winged, Slaty-backed gulls
Both Lesser and Greater Black-backed, I mull
Heermann's and Ivory, Yellow-footed too
But "Seagull" is not a bird I ever knew

That is not to say you're mistaken in full
Those various gulls, love the sea, if you will
So go ahead, call them Seagulls, if you must
Just remember their real names, as I've discussed
They're cousins but different, in that you can trust

Herrmanns Gull   Photo by Arthur Macmillan

California Gull

Ring-billed Gull   Photo by Becky Matsubara

Bonapartes Gull

Herring Gull

The Hermit Thrush is a winter visitor to Northern California, the only brown thrush regularly seen in North America during the winter months. It is a bird of the brushy understory of our pine and oak woods, making its living by scratching out insects from the forest's leafy floor. Gray-brown above, the Hermit Thrush's breast is heavily spotted. A white eye ring and rufous tail complete the picture. The similar looking Swainson's Thrush replaces the Hermit Thrush in the same habitat during the summer months. Among the avian world's finest singers, the thrushes' soft warbles and whistled phrases echo through the trees. Often hard to see in the forest's deep understory, their song lets you know they are there. Truly birds of the dense woods.

Photo by Becky Matsubara

Hermit Thrush

Bird of understory dark
in woods and forest dense
A faun, they say, in feathers clad
A bird of no pretense

Deep and dark your brushy home
Hides you from inquiring view
Only song affirms you're there
Attests that it is really you

Patience may allow a glimpse
Should you emerge from forest dim
Flicking wings and bobbing tail
Clear evidence that you are him

Should I live a hundred years
Ever should I be impressed
Melody of Thrush conveyed
Echoing o'er forest blessed

Photo by Becky Matsubara

Broken Wing Act   Photo by Arthur Macmillan

Killdeer are one of the larger members of the Plover group. Unlike their brethren normally seen along the coast as they migrate back and forth with the seasons, Killdeer prefer lake shores, plowed fields, pastures and lawns (always near water). They are quite noisy in flight. Their nests are built (if you want to call it that) on the open ground which makes them easily accessible to predators. While the nest and downy young tend to blend into the landscape, the Killdeer parents have nonetheless perfected the "injured wing" ploy to lure predators and other intruders away from the nest. The Killdeer is also the only large plover that does not develop a black neck and breast during the breeding season.

Killdeer

What is that plaintive dee, dee, dee I hear
From yonder pond so shrilly echoes out
It harshly and unkindly greets my ear
Designed to let all know that you're about

Denizen of pasture, lawn and field
A home you make so long as water's near
Your nest a shallow hole left unconcealed
Of predators, this bird seems not to fear
A type of larger plover --- the killdeer

So different from your kindred souls thou art
They when breeding, black turn neck and breast
Your two brown rings on neck set you apart
A smokescreen too when threatened near your nest

Red Fox lurking mutely in the Reeds
Mother, the protector of the nest
Loud as if on broken wing proceeds
To lure said fox, deter him from his quest

I see you often near old Lake Cascade
In fresh plowed fields whose seeds have yet to sprout
On grassy playing field where children play
Where e'er you are there surely is no doubt'
I'll hear that dee, dee, dee, you'll oft belt out

Photo by Becky Matsubara

The Lazuli Bunting visits Northern California during the spring and summer months. It is a bird of weedy open fields, often seen singing atop a thistle stalk. The stunningly beautiful sky-blue head and back of the breeding males, reminiscent of the color of Lapis Lazuli, give this bird its name. Dubbed the "Beautiful Sparrow" by early ornithologists. Females are a drabber sandy brown, with a bit of buff on their breast.

A cool fact about this bird from the Cornell Lab of Ornithology:

"Just like we each have our own voice, each male Lazuli Bunting sings a unique combination of notes. Yearling males generally arrive on the breeding grounds without a song of their own. Shortly after arriving, they create their own song by rearranging syllables and combining song fragments of several males. The song they put together is theirs for life."

Drawing by Nick Vaughn

Lazuli Bunting

Most beautiful of sparrows spry, Head blue, the color of the sky
Splotch of fiery orange on breast, sets you apart from all the rest

Warbling song from brushy tract, 'tis beautiful but not exact
To what your forebears tried to teach, but still alluring in the breach

I hear the song and hope to see, the singer belting out his plea
Urgent, pressing in hopes that soon, a fancier might hear his tune

A mile apace I come to hear, another warbling song that veers
But slightly from that heard before, a second warbling paramour

Now two admirers come to play, which of their songs will win the day
Each song enticing in its tone, but only one and one alone
Will win the heart each seeks to own

A year has passed, it's spring again, I trod through selfsame field and glen
And strain to hear a likened song, to wonder whether it belongs
To those who last year sang so strong, in hopes of finding love erelong

And soon I hear that lovely strain, similar but not quite the same
But close enough so that I know, that last year's singer found a beau

Again, the urgent ardent plea, from warbling bird makes clear to me
That nature's way, it's understood, is working still and life is good.

There are certainly more Lesser Goldfinch in my neighborhood than any other species of bird. On one occasion, I counted over 30 of these Goldfinch either at my feeders or waiting in the trees for their turn to feed. They love the abundant seeds from our Alders and the thistle seed I provide.

Photo by Arthur Macmillan

Lesser Goldfinch

Clinging high in Alder branches
Alder's seed pods bursting forth
Clear that you're in Goldfinch heaven
Nature's gift from bounteous earth

Winter comes and seedlings falter
You must find some other source
I am happy to oblige you
Nourishment to stay the course

You fight for shares at thistle feeder
Of't there's ten or twelve of you
More than any other species
Working hard to get your due

Less showy than your brighter cousin
With greenish back and duller breast
You're everywhere throughout my garden
Seeming ne'er in need of rest

My place would seem quite dull without you
So many grace my deck, my wall
Or splashing in the fountain near
Placed there for flyers one and all

I know you breed in this fair place
Come spring your numbers tell it all
Fledges flutter in the treetops
Wait to hear their parent's call

My home would be a lesser place
Were you not there to comfort me
My hoped-for presence dawn through dusk
To see you there, so calm, carefree

Shovelers are among the dabbling ducks. Most dabblers feed in the shallows of lakes and ponds by dipping their heads in the water with their tail straight up as they forage for small crustaceans and plant material. Shovelers are a bit different in that they swim across the shallows with their long, rather odd-shaped bill open and partially submerged to scoop up food as they swim. Dabblers will also occasionally forage on land for seeds, nuts, grains and insects. They will eat just about anything. Shoveler's white bodies are splotched with rusty side patches and a dark green head. The females, as with most duck species, are basic brown. Shovelers are winter visitors at the lakes and ponds near my patch—stopping for a rest on their way to their breeding grounds.

Northern Shoveler

As winter nears and you are flying through
my hood, whereat you see a patch of blue
And deign to take a rest from your long flight
To stop and fatten up for coming plight

Largest of the Dabblers you do float
Effortlessly as like a sailing boat
Pushed by a strong and steady breeze
You navigate the pond with greatest ease

Among the other dabblers you stand out
Most unusual is your extended snout
Detracts not one whit from your lovely frame
Emerald head and rusty sides acclaim
In looks you put most other ducks to shame

But most unique your elongated bill
A testament to Darwin, if you will
Enables you to feed where others don't
A gift from God to you and you alone

So don't belittle those who suffer you
For truth be told they haven't got a clue
Your longish bill from God was heaven sent
And you no reason have for discontent
As he who taunts, a crab, a malcontent

White-breasted Nuthatch   Photo by Becky Matsubara

Northern California has three species of Nuthatches—White-breasted, Red-breasted and Pigmy. Their names describe them perfectly, something I believe I need not belabor. They all thrive in the woods although the White- and Red-breasted Nuthatches prefer the large Valley Oaks that pervade much of the nearby countryside while the Pigmy Nuthatch prefers coniferous forests. All are distinguished by their ability to move down branches, tree trunks, garden walls, etc., head first. They feed basically on seeds and insects which are abundant in our area.

Red-breasted Nuthatch   Photo by Becky Matsubara

The Nuthatches

I am so lucky as to see, species of Nuthatches three
Two deciduous woods prefer, the third one opts for pines and firs
Both types do grace my home surrounds, so all three species can be found
short walk or drive from my abode, to where said Nuthatches have showed
Their presence for me to behold

If ever you should have a chance, see Nuthatch navigate a branch
The only bird to walk head first, down branch or wall to quench its thirst
or target seed or insect which, contains nutrition that is rich
in nutrients the Nuthatch needs, that will inexorably lead
to help the bird in life succeed

Most common in my neighborhood, White-breasted who is very good
at putting himself on display, nearby my fountain where he waits
'til other birds have drunk their fill, then inches down to where the swirl
of bubbling water waits for him to take a draught or a quick swim
To cleanse his feathers, keep them trim

Red-breasted even shyer still, he'll cling below our windowsill
Awaiting chance to quickly dart, to grab a sunflower and depart
before another bird's approach, who from Red-breasted oft might poach
That precious seed he's worked so hard to from the other birds keep guard

Of all the three the smallest is, the Pigmy Nuthatch who's a whiz
at plucking seeds from pine cones high, atop the tree where tree meets sky
Oft chattering with brethren clan, whose "bep, bep, bep" firmly commands
Attention from those down below, bird's calling card to let us know
To raise our eyes to see the show

So if you find yourself alone, in woods of varied tree-types known
You see a bird in treetop high, head down a branch as to defy
the forces nature has in place, creatures for to move with grace
A Nuthatch you have surely seen, so think not that you should demean
What for this bird is quite routine

Pygmy Nuthatch   Photo by Becky Matsubara

The Nuttall's Woodpecker's range is restricted to California and a tiny bit of the Baha Peninsula of Mexico. It is a year around resident. I have had a pair of these beautiful birds come to my feeders every year since I started placing feeders around the house. They are playful and fun to watch.

Nuttalls Woodpecker (female)

Nuttalls Woodpecker (male)   Photo by Becky Matsubara

Nuttall's Woodpecker

I see you through my office window
On the tree branch ahead
Near where I put out corn
for the squirrels
The suet feeder just below
Your target for a meal

You work your way slowly
down the trunk
to where the suet sits
Oft backing down the lowest branch
A watchful eye out for rivals
You feed from front or back
It matters not to you
I prefer the front so I can see
The delicate white stripes
across your coal black back

You are the Mother bird
Your crown also black and white,
echoing your back
I've seen you and your mate
Sometimes jockey for position
on the feeder

He with the red patch
at the base of his crown
A gentleman, he often waits
'til you have had your fill
Before he moves in
To take his turn

In the trees behind the house
I hear the tap tap tap
as you excavate for insects
beneath the bark
Your rattling call points me to the place
Where you are hard at work
Then our feeders beckon
filled with sunflower hearts
One of your favorites

Of all the Woodpeckers near my home
You are my favorite
Delicate yet playful
You and your mate
Never leave me
My Woodpecker friends

Photo by Becky Matsubara

The Oak Titmouse is one of four titmouse species found in the U.S. but the only one residing in my part of California. It is a small, grayish brown bird with beady black eyes and a crest it extends when excited. It is abundant in the Oak and similar trees found within its range. While other birds that come to my feeders often perch there for some time eating as much as they can in one sitting, the Oak Titmouse tends to dart to the feeder, grab a single seed, take it back to a safe perch somewhere on a tree, and eat it before returning for a second seed.

Oak Titmouse

Small, gray, mouse-like, I guess
From feeder back and forth
One seed each trip, no more no less
Just one and nothing more

Home in Western Live Oak trees
Pluck insects from the bark
Supplement with varied seeds
From gardens near, or park

Crest extended when excited
Not when things are calm
Diligent you, and farsighted
You work with poise, aplomb

Your song is wide and varied
I often need some time
Because you sound like others
Almost a perfect mime

So go about your business
It's back and forth you go
Yourself and fledglings happy
As fervently you stow
What they will need to grow

"Peeps" refers to the smallest of the sandpipers that travel up and down both our east and west coasts as they migrate back and forth from their breeding grounds in Northern Canada and Alaska. They include the Western, Least and Semipalmated Sandpipers. None is larger than 6 ½ inches in length. While sometimes solitary, the Least and Western Sandpipers are most often seen in large flocks that could consist of several hundred birds. The Semipalmated Sandpiper is mainly an East Coast bird but is seen sporadically along our West Coast. To see a large flock of Least or Western Sandpipers lift off together from a coastal sandbank, circle together in the air and return to where they started is a sight to behold.

Photo by Doug Mosher

The Peeps

The tide gone out, their moment has come
Creatures exposed in the black soft sand
Suddenly now, work all have begun
Heads bobbing wildly as the Peeps plumb
Feasting on whatever food is at hand

Then as the tide, slowly comes in
Hundreds of Peeps gather as one
Nestled together with heads tucked in wing
Settled to rest, no longer a din
'til the next tide, their foraging done

Lest an intruder foils the plan
Then to the sky they soar once again
Soaring and dipping in unison grand
Hundreds of Peeps alive o'er the land
'til danger gone their peace they regain

The cloud that I see far off yonder bank
Not filled with moisture plucked from ocean blue
Moving too fast, as it dips and banks
Surely alive as it moves in close rank
Ebbing and flowing it comes into view

Whirring of wings as the dark cloud comes near
Undulates, gyrates in unison flow
Deluge of sound catches one's ear
Approaching throng a black and white blear
Then settles down on the mudflat below

Least Sandpiper   Photo by Becky Matsubara

Western Sandpiper   Photo by Doug Mosher

Brown Pelican Diving   Photo by Doug Mosher

There are two species of Pelicans that live in the San Francisco Bay Area—Brown Pelicans and American White Pelicans. The former are denizens of the coastal waters—often seen flying along the coast in formation, inches from the water, and then rising up and diving headlong into the water to catch small fish. Their cousins the American White Pelicans favor fresh water. They fish in small groups, herding fish into the shallows of lake or pond and then scooping them up in their large bills.

The Pelicans

How similar, yet how different, these two cousins are
The divisions seem greater than likeness by far
Each with long bills, large pouches, majestic in flight.
But one of them brown and the other quite white

When full grown Mr. Brown's bill glows yellow and red
The yellow extending to the top of his head
A mature Mrs. White's bill of bright yellow glows
Black patches on wings Mrs. White proudly shows

In their manner of fishing, disparity reigns
The Browns hunts from above, strung out like a chain
Then dive to the water again and again
With bills open wide, they quickly lay claim
To the fish in their pouch, a reward for their pain

The Whites' preference is to hunt from below
They form a small group that proceeds very slow
They drive fish ahead until shallows are reached
Then together they plunge their large bills in the deep
And scoop up their dinner as their bounty they reap

When time comes for resting, again they depart
One in community, the other apart
Mr. Brown likes the rocks, on an island preferred
Amongst cormorants, seagulls, large numbers of birds
Where much grunting and croaking and squawking is heard

Mrs. White likes the quiet a sandbar provides
Only their brethren, none other resides
Away from the noise where there simply aren't any
But those of their kind, away from the many

The fact that these cousins so differently look
Their difference in fishing and mien they won't brook
Beckons well to the birder more interested she
To parse through not-so-subtle divisions to see
The wonders of nature, evolution set free

White Pelicans fishing   Photo by Doug Mosher

Brown Pelican   Photo by Becky Matsubara

Peregrine Falcon   Photo by Peter Shen

I am lucky to live in a spot where the Peregrine Falcon can be seen. It is a most beautiful bird. It is also a deadly predator, known for its speed and agility, always attacking from above. I have seen places nearby where these birds breed. I have also experienced a most exciting day on an Eagle count one January that provides fodder for this poem.

Peregrine Falcon

I see you in the pock-ed craggy heights of Castle Rock
Or atop the Inn at Seaside, where flights of pigeons flock
It really doesn't matter whether city, town or wild
So long as it is high above the clamor of mankind

For some time back we thought that you might soon become extinct
Extensive use of pesticides had put you on the brink
But lesson learned some laws were changed to help you make your way
And now you thrive so from today your cause we'll not betray

Your speed is legendary, you're the fastest of your kind
No bird can match your quickness, you leave all of them behind
From high above you set your sights, prey ignorant below
With folded wings, you streak t'ward earth outstretched to make the blow

Fond memories of winter past, a search for Eagles we
In boats upon a reservoir, we'd scope the distant trees
No eagles did we see that day but fortune it was ours
As Peregrine put on a show we'll ne'er forget for years

From tower left to tower right, said bird swooped o'er our boat
Three times it pierced the air above as it hurtled to and fro
The final time its target clear - a raft of Coots beyond
A sudden splash, the water roiled, the Coot did quick respond

This Coot will live another day, a lucky bird was he
The Peregrine who lost this time from water struggled free
We on the boat with mouths agape won't soon forget this day
When natures fastest animal for us was on display

The Red-necked and Wilson's Phalaropes are small sandpipers seen on both salt and fresh water ponds during their migration. They are even quite happy foraging on the settling ponds at our local sewage plants. We generally see them in California in the winter when they are in their duller non-breeding plumage. They can be seen swimming and spinning around on calm waters picking off insects from the water surface as they spin—a strange dance indeed.

The Phalaropes

Long distance travelers, just passing through
Need an occasional rest to refuel
Before moving on to breeding grounds north
Where your next generation will surely spring forth

In dull winter plumage, spring colors to come
Looking for places where insects abound
You settle on estuary, pond, lake or bay
To begin your strange dance, an exotic display

Spinning and twirling as if in a craze
Like pixies on water you daintily chase
Any poor insect that deign comes your way
For these Phalaropes, a gourmand's buffet

Some folk say a whirling dervish are you
Having seen you perform, I attest it is true
But no matter how comically droll it may seem
Your dance is effective, virtuoso supreme

Photo by Peter Shen

The Pileated Woodpecker is the largest of America's woodpeckers. It is more common in the Midwest and on the East Coast, but a few are permanent residents of woods along the northern California coast. Pileated Woodpeckers are the closest living relative to the Ivory-billed Woodpecker, a bird of the southern marshes thought to be extinct. I recently saw a pair of Pileated Woodpeckers at a nest hole in Redwood Regional Park—part of the extensive East Bay Regional Park System. This poem relates that experience.

Pileated Woodpecker

What is that boisterous "rap, rap" I hear
Sharp but not readily known to my ear
Surely a woodpecker working a tree
Too intense a Downy or Nuttall's to be
Need to get closer, need to get near

There high atop that snag of dead pine
Clearly a nest hole, clearly a sign
Pecker of wood is somewhere nearby
Patience required and we soon shall espy
Our lucky day—our stars have aligned

There from the hollow soft rapping is heard
Head of its tenant, from entrance emerged
Red crest aflame, Intense at its work
Spitting out wood chips and then with a jerk
Back in the nest so more shavings to purge

Soon from the forest amidst throbbing wings
Another with red crest to hollow hole brings
The soft leaves and grasses that make house a home
Time for observers to leave pair alone
Would that a family emerges come spring

Were your bill ivory rather than gray
Shadow of past – a ghost bird they say
Lost to the world, we'll see them no more
You a reminder of what came before
Of what we need do, to avoid a replay
Forestall such loss, keep extinctions at bay

The Pine Siskin—one of my favorite birds. Streaked brown with faded yellow wing bars and a short, pointed bill. Nothing particularly special about the look of these birds, but interesting that they are here at all. Pine Siskins were rare until suddenly one year they came to my thistle feeders in droves. An irruption they call it. In other years, sometimes they will come, but only when driven south by food or other climate conditions.

Pine Siskin

For years and years you never graced
The many feeders I have placed
Throughout my garden, deck and wall
For feathered friends both large and small

But now, come fall most every year
Almost like clockwork you appear
Your winter home now does extend
Brings my fair city, hence, a friend
Beginning of, I hope, a trend

In size like closest relative
The goldfinch, by whose side you live
Though only faintest yellow shows
In wing-and tail, both juxtaposed
'gainst streaks of brown from tail to nose

Come early spring you're gone again
To Northern breeding grounds I feign
We hope you'll come again next year
Like clockwork hope you'll reappear
Your presence we'll again endear

The Red-breasted Sapsucker is relatively common in our area but rarely seen. They get their name from their feeding habit of drilling holes in certain trees and waiting for the tree's sap to fill the holes. They then return for the sap and any insect that might have gotten trapped in that sticky stuff. They also feed on berries at times. This poem is based on an event that I experienced recently when a Red-breasted Sapsucker spent several days in a Privet Tree adjacent to my back deck.

Red-breasted Sapsucker

To where have you flown; I miss you so
Your appearance as sudden and unexpected
as your departure
It's been years since you were last seen here,
and then only once, on the Birch by the gate
Only then did I notice the neat rows of holes
carved in the tree's trunk
The flowing sap a source of nourishment
as well as a trap
for the many insects you will need
to feed open mouths come spring

But now you've come for neither sap nor insects
but for a different treat
The ripening berries on the Privet by the deck
So plentiful they bend the tree's branches
to the breaking point
A feast for the resident Robins, Waxwing,
and now for you
Why have I not seen you here before
at this annual blossoming of berries
No mind, you are here now and I am delighted

Each day for a week,
I rush to see if you have returned,
and you don't disappoint
The bright red on your head and breast
confirm that it is you
You rest while the Robins come and go
and, when they have left,
it is time for you to feast
And feast you do,
filling yourself with purple beads
bursting with nourishment

Then suddenly you are gone.
Have you had your fill?
Or is something else pulling at you
telling you it is time to move on
I may never know

But when my Privet blossoms next year
and explodes in purple fair
I'll rush to see if you've returned
In hopes that you'll be there

House Finch   Photo by Becky Matsubara

Four red finches are seen from time to time in California, but only two are what I would call "regular" residents of the East Bay of San Francisco. They are the ubiquitous House Finch and the less common Purple Finch. The House Finch is seen virtually everywhere, whereas it is a particularly good day of birding when a Purple Finch is seen. The red that forms on various parts of the male finches is due in large part to the variety of seeds, insects and berries the birds eat. On rare occasions, a change in diet can result in either orange or yellow substituting for the normal red seen on these finches.

The Red Finches

One a year-round resident throughout this land of ours
Familiar common House Finch, resides from shore to shore
The other hugs our western coast, no vagabond be he
The Purple Finch by all account, most difficult to see

The red is what distinguishes the males of these two breeds
Awash on head and breast and rump, the ladies for to please
The major difference 'tween the two, extent of wash and streaks
The Purple Finch more colorful, on flanks the striping weak

House Finch (yellow varient)   Photo by Peter Shen

Infrequently when diets change, some oddities occur
The regal males so lordly, proud, do show off red no more
Instead, because of nature's quirk, a different hue is shown
The wash on head and breast and rump, of orange or yellow glows

When e'er I venture to those spots that nature lures me to
I always see a House Finch, sure as the sky is blue
To greet me on my venture of discovery and search
But see a Purple Finch and it's like heaven here on earth

These two have distant cousins that on occasion show their face
The Cassin's Finch seen time to time uncommon in this place
Or Common Redpoll only when she's simply lost her way
But House and Purple sisters seem forever here to stay

Common Redpoll   Photo by Becky Matsubara

House Finch (Orange Variant)
Photo by Doug Mosher

Purple Finch

Red-shouldered Hawk pair   Photo by Peter Shen

Red-shouldered Hawks are common in much of the east and along the west coast. In my humble opinion they are the most beautiful raptor in our area. Adults have a rufous breast and belly, with black and white bands on their flight and tail feathers. Their rusty-red scapular feathers (shoulder) give them their name. I recently was blessed with a pair of these Hawks in the pine trees behind my house, where they built a nest and fledged a chick.

Red-shouldered Hawk

That plaintive call I hear
Keeya, Keeya, Keeya
Repeated again and again
Coming from the Pines
behind the house
Seemingly inconsolable, suffering

That mournful sound
I should be sad,
but I am not
For it bespeaks new life

Sudden shadow dancing
toward the trees
Sun reflecting off mottled wings
Rustling at the nest
The two come together
The mournful crying stops
All is well

Photo by Peter Shen

Photo by Peter Shen

The Red-tailed Hawk is the most common hawk in the San Francisco Bay Area and probably the most widespread hawk in the United States. It is distinguished by its broad wings, short tail, mottled breast band and, of course, its red outer tail feathers. The Red-tails' broad wings let them rise to great heights on upward air currents, without ever beating their wings, where they can soar for hours. They build bulky nests on trees or cliffs where they raise their young.

Red-tailed Hawk

You soar high above
Carried by the wind
Effortless
No need to flap your wings
The currents hold you aloft
Until you are ready to land

From high above
You can spot the vole in the meadow
The rabbit hopping here and there
Your eyesight is keen
You miss nothing
God's gift to your survival

Broad wings and short tail
Help in the hunt
You are silent on approach
The end is swift
Today you will not go hungry

Most familiar of your family
Seen high aloft
Or perched on yonder tower
There for all to see
Then you spring to life
Red tail flashing in the sun
Lets us know that it is you

Each time I venture out to nearby hills
I look for you; you rarely disappoint
Top predator, your hunting gives me chills
Your ease of flight a vivid counterpoint
Ruler of the skies, you nature will anoint

Photo by Becky Matsubara

As a young boy growing up in Southern Wisconsin, I used to marvel at the numerous Red-winged Blackbirds in the fields just beyond our house. They were my favorite bird at the time, due primarily to the distinct red and yellow patch on the wings of the males. Of interest, the wing patch on California's Red-winged Blackbirds is pure red. A different species of Blackbird, the Tri-colored Blackbird, sports a red and white patch, but that is for another poem on another day.

Red-winged Blackbird

Beyond the fence in pasture green
Gurgling voices, sight unseen
Hidden deep in grasses tall
I recognize them from their call

Then suddenly in flurry wild
Rise up from hidden domicile
And fill the sky, blot out the sun
Then settle back from whence they'd come

The young boy watches all in awe
Such spectacle ne'er seen before
How wonderful for him to see
such creatures flying fast and free

Always an unruly flock
Often cling to branch or stalk
of reed or grass, their favored ground
To meet and mate and raise their young

As flock gyrates across the sky
Black swirls are seen as they speed by
Then flash of red as eyes detect
Bursts of crimson they collect
When off bird's wings the sun reflects

Young lad shall not forget this day
When his intent was just to play
But Nature interfered and so
His love of birds began to grow
Together there with Nature's pull

Photo by Peter Shen

Rails are secretive birds, living and hiding in the salt water marshes that ring the San Francisco Bay. The Ridgeway Rail is the largest of the three rail species that inhabit the Bay. We are fortunate to have them as the Ridgeway Rail is designated "endangered" on the Federal Government's Endangered Species List. During the Gold Rush of 1849, the then Clapper Rail, called by many the "Marsh Chicken," was hunted by the thousands by marketers who would sell them to the miners for food. Today, the Arrowhead Marsh near the Oakland Airport is one of the best places to see and hear Ridgeway Rails. During King Tides, these rails, along with their cousins the Virginia Rail and the Sora, are forced to higher ground where they may be seen.

Photo by Peter Shen

The Ridgeway (formerly "Clapper") Rail

Weird, ugly and endangered, some say
Hides in the pickleweed 'round Frisco's Bay
Called "Marsh Hen" by some due to its size
Long-legged, short-winged, this bird rarely flies

It hugs the salt marshes of inlets and bays
Long bill ever probing for invertebrate prey
Found in the mud where these birds choose to live
Happy are they for the bounty it gives

Gold Rush miners and habitat loss
Imposed on this bird a terrible cost
Rendered endangered much had to be done
To improve the bird's lot or soon there'd be none

Thankful we are for the many who strove
Determined to help, they came forth in droves
The Bay for to "save," make it more like it was
'fore man's quest for fortune, with all its faux pas
Made it too late to move forward the cause

The result of their work – what we have today
A place one can go to see Rails on the Bay
Ridgeways, Virginias and some Sora, too
The marshes cleaned up so where these birds were few
Their numbers are up, the salt marsh renewed

Now each winter season when moon is aligned
And King Tides occur leaving nowhere to hide
The Rails for a moment condescend to be seen
The birders do gather – you can tell by their mien
To each birder there, how much the Rails mean

The Ring-necked Duck is one of three similar "diving" ducks found in the San Francisco Bay Area. It is the only one of the three that prefers fresh water and can be found in our inland lakes and ponds. The other two—the Greater and Lesser Scaup—prefer salt water. The Ring-necked Duck breeds in Canada but passes through the Bay Area on its annual migration back and forth between Canada and the southern US and Mexico where it spends the winters. Fortunately for we Northern Californians, some of these Ducks also spend much of the winter along the coast, including the inland areas of California, Oregon and Washington. The male of the species is a quite beautiful black and white bird. The female, alas, is a less distinct brown. While other species of waterfowl sometimes pass over my favorite local ponds during their migration without stopping, the Ring-necked Ducks never fail to make an appearance.

Ring-necked Duck (showing ring)   Photo by Peter Shen

Ring-necked Duck

How handsome you are,
All black and white
but for those yellow eyes
They call you "Ring-necked,"
but I see no ring
On the base of your bill, yes
but not on your neck
Oh well, they'll call you what they will

You love the local inland ponds,
Lake Cascade, the pond at Heather Farm
Unlike your sisters the Scaups
that prefer the Bay with its salty water
Less bright and colorful than you

I watch your comings and goings each year
Pretty much gone in the summer
Then returning in the fall
as you begin to head north
Where you breed
Sometimes over a hundred of you
on tiny Lake Cascade

You're taking a rest, fattening up
For the long journey ahead
to Canada
Where you'll raise your family
I'm glad you stopped by along the way
I would be disappointed if you had not

Cruising the western flyway north
The Teal, Widgeon, Bufflehead and you
A few by my local pond will stop
Some years the others will my pond eschew
Ring-necks, without fail, I can count on you

My father bought me a 16-gauge shotgun when I turned 16. As the County's only realtor at the time, Dad knew all the farmers within a few miles of our town and had permission to hunt on their land. In the fall, after the corn had been harvested and the corn stalks were left in the fields to dry, we would hunt for Pheasants in the corn fields.

Photo by Becky Matsubara

Ring-necked Pheasant

Autumn in Wisconsin
The air is crisp and the sky clear
The most beautiful time of year in these parts
The corn has been harvested
But the stalks are still in the field and turned
   brown
I trudge through the field with Dad,
three rows to the side
My new shotgun over my shoulder

Suddenly, a rustle ahead
Our dog stiffens to alert
Then the loud shutter of wings
A pheasant bursts forth
I raise my gun to shoot, but stop
It is a hen
I am almost glad
This marvelous bird will be safe today

Years later, hunting long gone from my mind
My shotgun securely stored in the loft
I see the pheasant quite differently
Most beautiful of all upland and field game birds
Iridescent green head, red mask and long tail
make the male unmistakable
Go ahead and strut, you have earned the right

I now live in the suburbs
I haven't walked through a corn field in years
And if I did, I would not be carrying a gun
Instead, my most precious of possessions
Those Zeiss binoculars
The flushed pheasant need not worry
I am only there but to gaze
At these beautiful birds

The Ruby-crowned Kinglet is one of the smallest birds in the winter forest – a mere four inches from bill to tail. It is a rather drab bird except when it raises and shows its ruby crest when excited. Its small, sharp bill is used to glean insects from the leaves and branches of trees and bushes as it flits through its leafy winter home. Its cousin, the Golden-crowned Kinglet, leads a similar life but is far less abundant and not often seen in my East Bay community.

Photo by Becky Matsubara

Photo by Doug Mosher

Ruby-crowned Kinglet

Tiny bird of winter woods
Skittering through the leafy green
As you seek your livelihood
Wings aflutter as you would
Revel this supernal scene

Olive green with lighter breast
Crowned with brightest ruby patch
Seen only when an unsought guest
Excites our bird to raise its crest
Intruder knows she's met her match

One of two bright crested birds
Your Gold-crowned cousin rarely seen
But you more frequently are heard
When through the nearby woods you stir
And nature's generous gifts you glean

Your welcome chatter always makes
Travelers through your leafy realm
Turn to you, a double take
With hope in mind for traveler's sake
Your sight to see, be overwhelmed

The Ruddy Duck is one of the smallest ducks seen on northern California's lakes and ponds—a mere 15 inches in length. It is sometimes known as the "Stiff Tail" duck due to its habit of raising its short, stiff tail as it glides through the water searching for food. Ruddy Ducks are widespread across the globe but were first identified in Jamaica (hence the scientific name "jamaicensis"). In breeding plumage, the male's reddish-brown body, black cap and neck, and white cheeks are set off by its distinctive bright azure blue bill—a most beautiful site to see. The females of this small species are known for laying the largest eggs of any duck in relation to body size. Those naughty birds also sometimes lay their eggs in other species' nests and let them raise their progeny.

Ruddy Duck

Little diving duck I see
Know you mean so much to me
Gracing ponds in winter's pall
Brighten darkest days for all

Easy to identify
Stiff tail reaching for the sky
There in tightly clustered flock
Breeding garb a rufous smock

Bill of male, distinctive hue
In spring it glistens azure blue
Attracts the ladies so they say
The brightest ones will have their way

Our smallest duck and yet you lay
The largest eggs in all the Cay
Often times in other's nest
At parenthood you're not the best

Yet when to Heather Pond I fly
Seeing you reminds me why
Nature holds this grip on me
God given creations such as thee

Sanderlings are small sandpipers common along the California coast during the winter season. They have a reddish head and breast when breeding but, when seen in California, they are almost ghostly white but for some gray on their back. They feed on small crustaceans on sandy beaches, usually in small flocks—often seen running toward the sea as waves along the shore recede and then running back as new waves pound the shore. I guess the waves churn up some of their favorite prey.

Photo by Ray Rozema

Sanderling

Sanderling nimble, Sanderling quick
Sanderling skips through the tough tidal rip
First toward sea, then toward land
Picking out food bits from the roiling sand

Ghostly in color, fast on its feet
Entirely intent on its next tasty treat
Absence of fear as the waves crash ashore
Stays until sated with no need for more

Then off with its brethren to rest on the rocks
Voice kwip, kwip, kwipping as it rejoins the flock
There to await the flock's next need for food
When back to the shore, waves again to elude

Photo by Ray Rozema

This smallest of the Plovers nests on the sandy beaches along the west coast of the U.S. Snowy Plovers are threatened by loss of habitat and encroachment by humans. Only 6 ¼ inches long, these dull gray/brown and white birds blend into the sand such that one could almost step on one without knowing it was there. Conservation groups have cordoned off sections of many beaches in the hopes of created safe spaces for these precious birds, particularly during the breeding season.

Photo by Becky Matsubara

Snowy Plover

Tiny ball of feathers gray
Concealed by the sand
Struggle you to have your way
About your favored land

Motionless as we pass by
To remain unseen
Slightest move might catch the eye
Showcase where you've been

Ever is more difficult
To find a place to nest
Manful acts a great insult
Deter you from your quest

Yet you remain so resolute
Determined to survive
You persevere relentlessly
Intent to make a life

For you and others of your kind
Though tiny you may be
I'd bet a sou that you will find
Safe home that meets your needs
Your home abreast the sea

We are fortunate in San Francisco's East Bay to live near many lakes and small streams. Actually, the "lakes" I refer to are mostly reservoirs created years ago by damming creeks to provide drinking water and water for agriculture and recreational uses. As the reservoirs aged, reed beds built up along their shores— ideal homes for the Song Sparrow. In truth this sparrow can make its home almost anywhere in woods or near water, even along the shores of the Pacific Ocean not far from where I live. I think the Song Sparrow got its name because it seems to be singing all of the time, although more so in the spring as breeding approaches.

Photo by Becky Matsubara

Song Sparrow

At home near lake or stream
Or shrub near garden wall
Near marshy valley green
It matters not at all

Its song its namesake dear
Reverberates throughout
Oft loud, distinct and clear
So as to leave no doubt

Three short notes start its song
Long trill to follow on
Listen, it won't be long
'til sound you'll soon be drawn

When startled just a chip
Makes Sparrow's presence known
Oft hiding near the tip
Of reeds near waters flow

Dark mantle, crown striped gray
Breast streaking heavier still
Converge in core spot splayed
White throat beneath gray bill

Walks through Briones Hills
In reeds near water's edge
I listen for the trills
Songs that to me allege
New life is soon to fledge

I think that I should see
No fairer bird than thee
When nature beckons me
To lake or woods or sea

The call of the Steller's Jay is often the first and the loudest sound heard on a typical walk in any of the many parks of our area—a very loud "shek, shek, shek, shek." This Jay is a common denizen of the woods all along the West Coast and into Canada and Alaska, whether a small stand of deciduous trees or the vast forests along the Sierra and Cascade ranges. As I live in a semi-rural community with plenty of trees, the Steller's Jay is a regular visitor at our feeders. It usually comes to a feeder in twos or threes, scares away the other birds at the feeder, has its fill for a couple of minutes and then leaves. In and out, bingo. Its breast, back and crested-head are black. The rest of it appears blue. In actuality, the blue is not truly blue as blue pigment is rare in nature. The blue is rather an optical illusion, caused by the way in which light is reflected off the Jay's feathers.

Stellar's Jay

A Blue Jay" said my novice friend
And while I wished not to offend
I had to clarify because
To see one here would give me pause
As rare these parts as Mr. Clause

I start by saying it is true
It is a bird and it is blue
But this bird claims a different name
For Georg Steller of Alaska fame
First saw the bird and laid his claim

But wait, let's rethink for a sec
The blue on bird I must correct
Construction of the feathers makes
Sunlight reflect blue by mistake
Off feathers black, the blue a fake

Now happy throughout all the West
From coastal shore to mountain crest
His squawking cry heard from afar
So loud at times one's ears it jars
The quintessential fab rockstar

At first it seems a bully he
Appears to make his neighbors flee
From places where the food is placed
With wings aflutter, he does race
So he'll the morsel first to taste

But soon the prize so dearly earned
He moves aside, provides a turn
For those that wait so patiently
On garden wall or limb of tree
A gentleman, they'd all agree

So bothersome as Jay might sound
I say it's nice that he's around
To liven up the place a bit
When quiet to extremes it gets
I mind the noise nary a wit

Photo by Doug Mosher

Surf Scoters are sea ducks—never found in fresh water, except in the Midwest's Great Lakes. As their name suggests, they love the ocean surf and can be seen diving and cavorting in the surf all along the west coast of California during the winter months. At that time, these Scoters are migrating to breeding grounds in northern Canada and Alaska. While large numbers simply pass us by well off shore, a few can't resist the California surf and grace us with their presence. Males are all black except for a white patch on their forehead and an elongated white and orange bill, that has garnered for them the name of "Skunkhead Coot."

Surf Scoter

Coal black but for that droll bill and white patch
The pounding surf your playground
Despite its stout force the surf is no match
A detour on trip northward bound

As crashing waves do pound the sandy shore
You see a challenge firm
As wave behind you crests with mighty roar
Into its trough you squirm

Then pop you up on the waves other side
Completely free of harm
While we on the beach amazed and popeyed
View you with admiring charm

The ocean, feared and foreboding to some
To you a venue for play
You cavort in its shallows, its depths you do plumb
To you, just another day

Green-winged Teal

Cinnamon Teal Pair   Photo by Becky Matsubara

There are three species of Teal that grace us in Northern California—the Green-winged Teal, the Blue-winged Teal and the Cinnamon Teal. Each are beautiful in their own way. All are dabblers and with us only during the winter months. The Green-winged Teal is by far the most abundant. Blue-winged and Cinnamon are less common. The adult breeding males are distinct. It takes a sharp eye to distinguish between the rather drab mottled brown of the females.

The Teals

Green-winged, Blue-winged, Cinnamon, too
In our late fall you make your debut

Misters colorful, madams are drab
Lurk in pond's shallows where repasts you grab

Green-wing most abundant of all
And of all dabblers, you the most small

Blue-wing most exotic by far
Most birders think of you as the star

Fairest of the trio of teals
Cinnamon's glow, reflection appeals

Bragging rights to birders who say
Lucky was I, a three teal day

Blue-winged Teal Pair

Vultures are nature's clean-up crew. They can smell carrion from miles away and make quick work of it. During a trip to East Africa, I saw 40 or more vultures atop the carcass of a Water Buffalo. Our guide told us that in a few days not much would be left of that carcass. In Northern California, the resident vulture is the Turkey Vulture. Not much to look at with its featherless red face and all black body, but very efficient at its work. These birds can soar for hours looking for carrion. They nest in the hollow of large trees as I once frighteningly discovered.

Vulture Chicks in Tree Hollow

Photo by Arthur Macmillan

Turkey Vulture

Hollow tree I see up yonder, what could be its use I ponder
Might the tree be sick I wonder, or just a blight on tree's décor?
Must explore this hollow further, interesting it is, I murmur
Not to harm, just an observer, wondering what that hole is for
Think perhaps the tree is dying
Just some rot and nothing more

Carefully approach the hollow, filled with awe at what may follow
Overhead there banks a swallow as I near the hollow's door
As I stoop to look inside, vulture rushes passed my side
Freedom not to be denied, toward the sky the bird does soar
Perches she on highest limb
Know I that she me abhors

Once recovered from my fright, deep in hollow such a sight
Two young fledges fluffy, bright, sitting on the hollow's floor
Slowly I retreat a step, hoping not to overstep
Right I have to view the cleft, nature placed at hollows door
Mother watching patiently
Wants me gone for evermore

More to say re this short tale, parents gone so not to fail
Roam the skies on thermal sails, search for food a daily chore
Finding what the fledglings need, so they'll grow and soon be freed
From the hollow in the tree, take their place in nature's corps
Only then will fledglings two
Live the life created for

The Varied Thrush has haunted me ever since I took up bird watching. I saw one early in my birding days, thought it beautiful and continued to look for it thereafter. But it is elusive. I quickly learned that this Thrush tends to spend winters farther north. Only in exceptional years does it venture into my territory – when food or other factors drive it south. I continue each year to search for Varied Thrush and delight in seeing one when it graces me with its presence. In only one year, was this bird abundant.

Varied Thrush

See you each day where you preside
on the front cover of my field guide
Orange and black, your wings outstretched
Companion you as the hills I trek
But to find you in the countryside –
A different matter, friends confide
Your presence they say, will be denied

Most years you're nowhere to be seen
But now and then in deep ravine
You condescend, let presence known
Until next year, your cover blown
Then comes a year, you're everywhere
Food must be scarce up north this year
Forcing you to venture south
I'm happy to have you about

You love the dense dark of the woods
In canyon deep near where I stood
Carved o'er time by water fast
Near stream below where now I cast
My eyes to see you there below
But valley lined with Bay and Oak
And tangle of green undergrowth
Makes viewing hard, but then they say
You tend to like it just that way

And, when winter's scarce resources
drive you south o'er different courses
To see you now I need not strain
I drink in all of you I can
Flash of orange from throat and breast
Soak up each detail I with zest
I sit and stare 'til I've amassed
Of you all my mind will holdfast
For fear this time should be my last

Violet-green Swallows forage in groups but nest in cavities, sometimes including nest boxes. They are birds of cliffs and open fields, often near water, feeding on insects as they swoop overhead or near the ground. They are not a bird I would expect to see in a residential back yard. This poem is based on an event I experienced while sitting in my back yard in Orinda, California, soaking up sun and getting some rest. Before I knew it, the sky above was filled with a half dozen Violet-green Swallows which, for some reason, were transfixed by their own image in the upstairs windows of my home.

Photo by Becky Matsubara

Violet-green Swallow

As I sit and sun 'neath summer sky
The sound of wings disturbs my rest
I raise my eyes to see on high
A swirl of Swallows passing by
As from my peacefulness I'm wrest

I peer to get a better look
Swallows I see on cliffs, in fields
High in the hills, o'er pond and brook
Never have I by hook or crook
Seen Swallows where I from nature yield

Yet, here I am, my own backyard
Where many songbirds congregate
But Swallows from these places spared
Or could they be some false canard
Approach so my rest to frustrate

But wait, up there on window screen
A Swallow looks in window clear
Its back a shining violet green
With fluttering wings to me it seems
Into my home it hopes to veer

Time and again, the game plays out
To window screen and back again
This strange behavior leaves no doubt
What drives the bird to take this route?
Its image fair off window pane

I wish these birds would entertain
me every time I venture out
See them again? I think it's plain
Near brook and field they will remain
See here no more, I've little doubt

Great Blue Heron Photo by Becky Matsubara

The Great Blue Heron and the Great Egret are of the Genus Ardea. They are the largest of the wading birds found in Northern California. I am privileged to be near rookeries of these birds both in the East Bay where I live and near Monterey Bay where I often visit. The former is in a stand of Eucalyptus Trees near a utility-owned reservoir only a few miles from my home. The latter also favor Eucalyptus on, of all places, a dairy farm that abuts the Elkhorn Slough, an estuary out of Moss Landing located a few miles north of Monterey. I frequent both as much as possible. These birds hunt motionless in shallow water and spear their prey with powerful neck muscles and long pointed bills. During breeding season, the rookeries can be deafening.

The Waders
(Great Blue Heron and Great Egret)

Dwellers extant wherever water flows
Long-legged waders you
Largest of the birds Mother Nature chose
Ambush fishing to pursue

Silent hunters, your prey you slowly stalk
In shallow waters still
Long coiled neck, a snake primed to attack
With deeply gifted skill

Powerful neck and long dagger-like bill
A cannon fully charged
Your sudden strike, designed to make the kill
Your prey you do bombard

When spring's passions foretell the time is near
A rookery designed
From afar herons and egrets both appear
Now allies well aligned

Soon the trees alive with squawking chicks
Calling to be fed
Skills are tested, need be agile, quick
For the hunt ahead

Return you soon to mouths now opened wide
The silence is profound
This place where Herons and Egrets both reside
All well – joy abounds

Great Egret with prey   Photo by Peter Shen

Western Bluebird   Photo by Becky Matsubara

Western Bluebird feeding Fledge   Photo by Becky Matsubara

The Western Bluebird is one of three species of bluebirds in the U.S. An almost identical cousin, the Eastern Bluebird, resides throughout the U.S. east of the Rocky Mountains. The Mountain Bluebird resides, you guessed it, in the mountains—seen often throughout the Sierra Nevada Range. Western Bluebirds like the open spaces of the West, feeding primarily on insects they catch on the wing. They build their nests in holes in trees and are happy to accept residency in bird houses. The male Western Bluebird in breeding plumage is a stunning sight to see.

Western Bluebird

What was that flash of blue that crossed our path?
A hint of rusty red commingled with
Fair as a winged fairy gliding past
A glowing sapphire—is it real or myth

Most beautiful of birds you surely are
When glint of sun reflects your azure hue
Appear you then as if a blazing star
A gift to us most lovely through and through

Atop yon thistle stalk you shrewdly wait
'til hapless insect haps' to flutter near
Then off you fly, unflinching fast and straight
Your bill transformed into a deadly spear

You nest inside the home I made for thee
A simple box set off in yonder field
In hopes my gift perchance will grant to me
The chance a bluebird family revealed

Western Grebes are the largest of the Grebe species in the United States. They are common along the U.S.'s west coast in both salt and fresh water. They are noteworthy because of the fancy ritual mating dance that males and females engage in during the breeding season. First, they participate in a bobbing ritual that can go on for some time. Then, pushing themselves up in the water, they scoot across the surface, heads held high in perfect synchronization. Time and again, the dance continues. It is amazing to see, but it seems to work. Mating occurs soon after.

Western Grebes Mating Dance

Western Grebes

Alone one Sunday afternoon
Strolling past nearby lagoon
I hap'd to look at water blue
As sun o'er clouds came shining through

A pair of birds soon caught my eye
And while I am not one to pry
I thought that I should venture near
It being springtime of the year
To see what stirrings might appear

These birds decked out in black and white
Appeared engaged in sacred rite
One loudly calls, retort is heard
They then approach, their hearts strings stirred

First breast to breast and face to face
They make it clear they own this place
Should interloper come too near
He's placed himself in mortal fear

One lifts its head, then nimbly nods
And then without a push or prod
Its partner deftly does the same
An echo of her suitor's flame

Then dip to left and dip to right
Their head dips bring me much delight
Then separate a foot or two
And dipping and nods begin anew

But soon a faceoff does occur
A stare-down betwixt him and her
Their necks extended; bills held high
They're pointed upward toward the sky

Then suddenly, the waters churn
As he and she through water burn
Feet churning like propellers flay
Now side by side a fair ballet

They walk on water some folks say
More like a freight train gone astray
But I believe it to this day

Grebes Mating Ritual   Photo by Doug Mosher

Western Meadowlarks thrive in the abundant open grasslands of Northern California, which includes most of the 121,000 acres (73 parks with over 1,200 miles of trails) that make up the vast East Bay Regional Park System. These birds are beautiful singers—their gurgling whistle echoes over the meadows. While they are year-round residents, their songs are heard mostly during the spring and summer months when "love is in the air." Nothing beats a walk through a nearby park and hearing the sound of scores of Meadowlarks in full voice.

Photo by Bob Lewis

Photo by Bob Lewis

Western Meadowlark

Mysterious "Song of the Lark"
Inspiration for books, paintings and song
That of Cather, Breton, Tchaikovsky
The seduction of William's "Lark Ascending"
What magic hath thou wrought

Lovely Lark of California's meadows
Lurking unseen in the high grasses
Often hundreds strong, free from danger
Your songs ring out – music to our ears

Your symphony of song a sign of spring
Of rebirth, restoration, reawakening
Gladdens the heart of the passer by
Signals the fox, squirrel and coyote
The time to raise a family nears
To all other creatures, a sign that all is well

Lovely Lark of California's meadows
What power in a song
The power to evoke a smile and lighten our load
The power to let all know they are safe in the moment
Mysterious "Song of the Lark"
My inspiration, like Erato -- my muse

Song of the Lark, the last book in Willa Cather's *Great Plains Trilogy*; a work by Jules Adolphe Aimé Louis Breton hanging at the Art Institute of Chicago; and a march by Pyotr Tchaikovsky.

Photo by Becky Matsubara

The Western Screech Owl, like its eastern cousin, is a small owl, a night hunter, that nests in hollow cavities of large trees and roosts, often in plain sight during the daylight hours, in the same or smaller hollows. It frequents parks, suburbs and even deserts, as well as woods yet remains unseen by most who pass by. Its diet consists primarily of insects and small rodents. I presume it gets its name from the loud whistles it utters, accelerating to a short trill, followed by a longer trill.

Western Screech Owl

Park, town, field or wood,
you are there but rarely seen
For daylight hours its understood
A time for calm, to rest and preen

Ghostly night hunter, silent in your quest
Search the forest floor in hopes to find
Food sufficient for the needed task, lest
Chicks alone in hollow left behind
Their needs unmet, their confidence maligned

I see you not though know that you are near
When darkness falls, and ventures me outdoor
I hear the whistling trill that makes it clear
That you in nightly search as nights before
Your ghostly shadow graces me once more

As luck would have it, twice in my long life
Your presence on the roost was by me seen
Once in nearby woods, once in city rife
With many walkers strolling parkland green
Most pass by ne'er knowing where you've been
They pass on pathway close, you go unseen

I am writing this blurb on April 19 and just received a post that a fellow birder has this day seen her first Western Tanager of the season ("FOS" in birder speak). A sure sign that spring has arrived. While preferring cool conifer forests of the West's higher elevations, these Tanagers may be seen throughout California during the spring and fall migration. The male casts a stunning figure with its yellow breast, belly and rump; black back, tail and wings, with yellow wing bars; and bright red head. While Western Tanagers prefer to forage in the higher reaches of trees, the adult males are nonetheless hard to miss with their striking colors.

Photo by Bob Lewis

Western Tanager

First of the Season, comes the cry
Below the live oak tree
For there atop tree's branches high
Springtime's jubilee

Aphrodite in feathered garb
Most beautiful to see
Striking hues set you apart
None handsomer than thee

Your entrance keenly we await
Each springtime of the year
For on that day our joy is great
The day that you appear

Golden-crowned Sparrow   Photo by Arthur Macmillan

White-crowned and Golden-crowned Sparrows are our "winter" sparrows in Northern California. They breed much farther north and join us in early September. By the end of March or early April they are gone. They are the most abundant sparrows seen in the surrounding grassy hills, often in large flocks. They are also frequently seen around feeders in town—feeding primarily on the ground on seeds other birds have knocked off the feeders.

White- and Golden-crowned Sparrows

In far reaches of Canada you both were born and raised
But as the chills of fall approach, its warmer climes you crave
We're lucky that the two of you did choose to winter here
Our winter Sparrows, crown-ed both, a treat we hold most dear

No matter where I venture forth, on hill or deepest dale
Your presence always comforts me, your nature's holy Grail,
But should I find no signs of you, abundant as you are
My day and walk seem incomplete, you've left a tiny scar
on otherwise a perfect day, my dazzling avatar

Never solo, Mr. White, always in a group
Often ten or twenty of you making up your troop
Scratch, scratching on the ground, searching for your meal
Oblivious to passers-by unless they seek to steal
what your and fellow Mr. Whites scratch scratching has revealed

Crown your conclusive marker, stripes of white and black
'cept for recent fledges, for whom bold colors lack
As well as Mr. Brown and Tan, a relative be he
A "Mr. White" genetically, of black and white he's free

Now Mr. Gold's another thing, extensive black on head,
But when mature a golden patch atop the crown imbeds
While Mr. Gold like Mr. White feeds mainly on the ground
He is more apt than Mr. White on feeders to be found
Come March both Messrs. White and Gold, have left us northward bound

In great anticipation, I wait each fall and spring
For signs that my crowned sparrows have come or taken wing
Reminders of the seasons, these crown-ed sparrows are
In winter wonted presence; In summer off afar

White-crowned Sparrow   Photo by Becky Matsubara

White-tailed Kites   Photo by Becky Matsubara

A couple of years ago I was lucky to have a pair of White-tailed Kites build a nest and fledge four chicks in a clutch of Pines behind my home. These all-white birds with black shoulder patches and falcon-like wings are beautiful to behold. I submitted an article about my experience with the Kites to a birding magazine. They said they would publish it but I haven't seen it yet. So the story must be told in poetry.

White-tailed Kites

High atop the Diodora Cedar
I see you every afternoon
Surveying the open expanse
behind my home
A blaze of white,
Dark patches on your shoulders
What are you searching for?
Why are you here?

During treks in open space nearby
I sometimes see you
or your brother or your sister
Soaring overhead
Pointed wings outstretched
Riding the winds
You seem more at home there

Days go by before I see another like you
Far in the distance
It approaches warily
It lands atop a cedar near to yours
Now there are two of you
Could this be your mate?
He's there again today
and the next day and the day after that

The sun is out today
I check the cedars once again
They're there, on cedars side by side
He approaches. She rises up. They embrace
Then settle back upon their stately thrones

Ensuing days bring flurries of activity
No time to waste
They disappear and then return
with branch or twig in beak
Always to the same place
high in a Monterey Pine off to the west
Just beyond my view
Are they building a nest?

Days go by and I am nervous.
In a week's time I must leave
A long-planned visit overseas
Will I miss the climax
of one of nature's miracles?
The time has come and I must go
I bid adieu to my new friends

The plane touches down at SFO
I have been two weeks away
No thought given to my feathered friends
I am tired and am soon abed
The sun arises as the new day dawns
I step outside to breath fresh air
Off to my left the Diodora beckon

I marvel as atop the tallest of those trees
sit four fledged Kites
All white with black shoulder patches
Parents perched atop trees left and right
A fine family indeed
I have missed nothing
I am lucky, I am blessed

You are White-tailed Kites
Born to soar above open plains
Wings outstretched
Searching for insects or small rodents
to keep your internal engine firing
Perhaps I will see you again
When I roam the adjacent hills and valleys
I will be blessed again if I do
You most lovely of birds

Kite mating ritual – exchange of food in flight   Photo by Michael Bolte

Swifts are most unusual birds in that they are unable to perch on twigs or branches due to the configuration of their feet. Rather, they cling to the sides of cliffs (or the inside of chimneys in the case of Chimney Swifts) when roosting at night. Our White-throated Swifts spend all of their daylight hours in flight, twisting and turning at incredible speeds through the canyons and cliffs of the West to capture insects out of the air. Occasionally, they come down from the heights to get a drink. At Lake Cascade near my home, I have seen a single Swift skim across the water for a drink, never stopping. They are also known to follow farm equipment that kick up insects for a quick meal. But, for the most part, they stay aloft, even having sex while in flight.

White-throated Swift

High above the cliffs of Castle Rock
I see you in the morn and as eve' nears
In between you simply disappear
Foraging aloft amidst your flock

You revel in the clouds that pass us by
Home to gnats and spiders you adore
Snaring them in flight as high you soar
Through the daylight hours 'til night is nigh

Then return to crevice on cliff's wall
Cling to crevice walls amidst the throng
Of fellow roosting Swifts oft hundreds strong
Away from trace of man and human sprawl

When amorous pursuits are in the air
Two courting birds in sudden dive can oft
be seen together fall from sky aloft
Embraced in flight, accomplish their affair
Then swoop back skyward with a graceful flair

These Swifts, perhaps most graceful of their kind
Long arched wings the perfect flyer make
At home amid the clouds your claim you stake
Monarch of the air, by God designed

Wood Duck Pair Photo by Peter Shen

In my opinion, Wood Ducks are without question the loveliest of all Northern California ducks. The breeding male's tufted head a kaleidoscope of green, red, black and white. Its dark body offset by a large yellowish patch on each side. The duller female is nonetheless distinct in having a unique white eye patch surrounding her dark eye. Wood Ducks inhabit quiet streams, estuaries and swampy areas always staying close to water. While secretive and difficult to find, I did see 50 of them in a neighbor's pond during a recent Christmas bird count. What a stroke of good luck.

While wood ducks are considered dabblers, they are unusual in that they often perch high in the branches of trees near their watery patch, even nesting in tree cavities and nest boxes nailed to the trunks of trees, the only duck in our area to do so. And unlike other dabblers, Wood Ducks eat primarily acorns and seeds.

Wood Duck

Patchwork quilt of colors fair
Most pleasing of your kind
Of nature's hues you have your share
None more lovely will you find

On quiet streams you make your home
Or sheltered ponds or swamps
You never far from water roam
Your anchor, covert camp

Unlike your plainer dabbler friends
You a "percher" be
To go aloft pays dividends
Much safer all agree

While usually found in smaller groups
One day you did confound
When there two score and ten of you
Were seen in neighbor's pond

Suppose that I shall never see
You congregating so
I'll look for you in wilder parts
Where peaceful waters flow

Townsend's Warbler   Photo by Becky Matsubara

Wood Warblers are not a single species. They are what birders call that abundance of colorful warblers that migrate spring and fall through our woods and grace us with their presence. A few stick around either during our winter or summer seasons—the latter breeding and raising chicks near where I live. The Bay Area's most common winter Wood Warblers are the Yellow-rumped and Townsend's Warblers. During the summer months Wilson's, Yellow, Black-throated Gray and Orange-crowned Warblers call the Bay Area home. Many others are seen during migration. David Sibley's "Guide to Birds of Western North America" describes 42 Warbler species seen somewhere in the American West.

Wood Warblers

Elusive Warbler, foraging on high
Just passing through or might you stay awhile
Or spend with us the season if you will
Either summer's dog days or winter's chill

Oh, for trace of color midst the leaves
Or off your wing a glint of sun perceived
Burst of yellow, vivid red or olive green
Most oft' you seem to choose to go unseen

You flit and fly so quickly through the tree
Most difficult you make for me to see
Whether traveling Warbler passing through
Or of these woods a resident bird who
Will linger and a family life pursue

I wonder why so fascinated we
These songbirds, so small, so hard to see
Perhaps it is their colors, bright and rich
Wood Warblers they, they hold a special niche
Wood Warblers they—we birders can't resist

Wilson's Warbler   Photo by Becky Matsubara

Orange-crowned Warbler   Photo by Becky Matsubara

Yellow Warbler   Photo by Doug Mosher

Yellow-rumped Warbler   Photo by Bob Lewis

The Yellow-rumped Warbler is our most common winter warbler—nick-named "Butter Butt" by birders because of its yellow rump. It is a sweet little wood warbler that forages from trees, on fence posts and from the ground—often darting out from its perch to snag an insect and then flying back from whence it came. While the majority of Yellow-rumped Warblers also have yellow throats, a small "Myrtle" population have white throats. Come spring, the Yellow-rumps are gone—headed north or to higher elevations for the spring and summer seasons where they breed and raise families.

Yellow-rumped Warbler

Sweet little "Butter Butt"
Cute little "Butter Butt"
Foraging high up above
You're called Mr. Butter Butt
Due to your yellow rump
Common but surely beloved

Here in our winter time
Colorful in your prime
Yellow on throat, rump and wings
Chip chipping all the time
Flitting from oak to pine
Magnificat when you sing

Plan for next meal is hatched
Dart out and quickly snatch
Insects that fly near your perch

An expert, you make the catch
Insect is soon dispatched
Then it's on to the next search

Very sporadically
Lucky am I to see
Butter Butt throated in white
Same self society
Of Myrtle variety
Birders enthralled by the sight

Come springtime you disappear
Gone for another year
Headed up north so to breed
But come fall it is clear
You will soon reappear
'til then we wish you Godspeed

Afterword

If you have finished *Poetry Takes Flight* and are already a birder, I hope that you enjoyed at least a few of the poems and that I didn't grossly misrepresent either the characteristics or antics of any of the birds featured.

If you finished the book and are new to birding, I hope that the poems will further stimulate your interest in our fascinating feathered friends and encourage you to spend more time in the hills or woods near you.

If reading *Poetry Takes Flight* is your first foray into the life of birds, I hope that a poem or two may have piqued your interest in learning more about birds or, at least, paying more attention to what you see when you venture outdoors.

At the very least, I hope that one or two of the poems "tickled your fancy" or made you think a bit about the subjects of the poems (in this case the marvels that are birds). For, after all, isn't that what poetry is all about.

About the Author

For the last half century, Jim Roethe has lived in Orinda, California, an East Bay suburb of San Francisco, where he has hiked and birded in the hundreds of miles of trails that are part of the East Bay Regional Park system and the local water utility.

Jim is a member of the Golden Gate Audubon Society, and for the last several years he has led the North Orinda Christmas Bird Count for the Society. He also has participated in Christmas counts in other areas of both the East Bay and the Monterey area where he maintains a second home.

Jim is a semi-retired attorney who still serves as an arbitrator from time to time. In addition to his interest in birding, Jim loves traveling (he has traveled in every continent except Antarctica) and has sung in a number of choirs in the East Bay. He also has written several books about family, travel and birds.

While he has dabbled in poetry over the years, *Poetry Takes Flight* is Jim's first published book of poems. His hope is to inspire readers to look around them when outdoors, see the wonderful world of birds, and gain an understanding of what inspires so many today to take up birding.